Praise fo

"Blessed Teresa of Calcutta considered *Union with God* to be her favorite work from which she drew great solace... Mother Teresa would quote from him extensively, even citing him in her original hand-written copy of the *Constitutions of the Missionaries of Charity*...

This work is a collection of letters of spiritual direction which only can be described as being very simple yet very deep, encouraging childlike confidence in God as our loving Father. Blessed Columba's letters simplify the complexities of life and helped his spiritual directees stay focused on what Jesus was asking of them in the present moment."

—David L. Toups, S.T.D., *writing in the Foreword*

"This book is pure gold. I started highlighting parts of the book when I came upon profound spiritual passages, but soon determined I would save time by simply dying the pages of the book yellow. So much of the book truly resounded with me and stayed with me throughout the day as I used this book as spiritual reading in the morning. Marmion is able to put things so well that they really broke through to me even when I was pretty much aware of the basic idea of what he was saying before. As always there is a great distance from head knowledge and truly understanding something with your heart.

I could not recommend this book more highly."

—Jeff Miller, *The Curt Jester weblog*

"Superb!!! I've read spiritual books for 35 years. This is the greatest of them all! It makes me feel united to Jesus!"

—L.J.K. (Flint, Michigan)

"Wise advice about prayer and spiritual growth, virtues and perfection, temptation and trials, detachment and devotion. No wonder this was a favorite book of Blessed Teresa of Calcutta."
—Paul Thigpen, *The Catholic Answer*

"Truly, this is an inspiring, hope-giving work. For those of us in the trenches, who seem like we never move forward, Dom Columba raises the battle cry that will jolt us out of complacency and send us forward."
—Steven Riddle, *Flos Carmeli weblog*

"One of the most beautiful books you can read, and reread many times! I just ordered one dozen *Union with God* to share this great gift with as many people as I can."
—Valdemar Welz, D.M.D. (Boston, Massachusetts)

"This book is like having your own Spiritual Director with you. As a Secular Order of Discalced Carmelite, I recommend this book for anyone wishing for spiritual direction."
—A.J. (New Orleans)

"This is an exceptional book. Dom Marmion's insight, wisdom, compassion and simplicity are deeply moving."
—R.K.R. (Long Island, New York)

"One word: Outstanding. The spiritual advice he gives is applicable to all people, like St. Francis de Sales' writings."
—L.M.

"It is so awesome to have Blessed Marmion's writings back in circulation! Thank you for publishing these writings so important to the Catholic Church. May we all continually grow deeper in our 'Union with God'."
—V.T.S. (St. Paul, Minnesota)

Union with God

BOOKS BY

Blessed Columba Marmion

Christ, the Life of the Soul

Christ in His Mysteries

Christ, the Ideal of the Monk

Christ, the Ideal of the Priest

The English Letters of Abbot Marmion

Words of Life

Sponsa Verbi

Union with God

Letters of Spiritual Direction
by Blessed Columba Marmion

Selected and Annotated by
Dom Raymond Thibaut

Translated by
Mother Mary St. Thomas

ZACCHEUS PRESS
Bethesda

Nihil Obstat: Censores deputati

Imprimatur: P. Cawet, *Episc. coadjut.*
              Namurci, December 8, 1934

ZACCHEUS PRESS and the colophon are trademarks of Zaccheus Press. The
Zaccheus Press colophon was designed by Michelle Dick.

The text is set in Fournier.

Library of Congress Cataloging-in-Publication Data
Marmion, Columba, Abbot, 1858-1923.
    [Union with God according to the letters of direction of Dom Marmion]
    Union with God : letters of spiritual direction by Blessed Columba
Marmion / selected and annotated by Dom Raymond Thibaut ;
translated by Mother Mary St. Thomas.
       p. cm.
    Originally published: Union with God according to the letters of
direction of Dom Marmion. London : Sands & Co., 1934.
    Includes index.
    ISBN-13: 978-0-9725981-6-3 (pbk. : alk. paper)
    ISBN-10: 0-9725981-6-2 (pbk. : alk. paper)
    1. Marmion, Columba, Abbot, 1858-1923—Correspondence. 2. Spiritual
direction. 3. Spirituality. I. Thibaut, Raymond, b. 1877. II. Title.
    BX4705.M411A4 2006
    248.4'82—dc22

                                                    2006030051

10 9 8 7 6 5 4 3 2

To learn more about Blessed Columba Marmion, please visit our webpage:

www.zaccheuspress.com

TABLE OF CONTENTS

FOREWORD
by
Rev. David L. Toups, S.T.D.

UNION WITH GOD was first compiled ten years after Abbot Columba Marmion's death in 1923, and then, as now, it brilliantly captures his insights into the spiritual life. This work is a collection of letters of spiritual direction which only can be described as being very simple yet very deep, encouraging childlike confidence in God as our loving Father. Blessed Columba's letters simplify the complexities of life and helped his spiritual directees stay focused on what Jesus was asking of them in the present moment. His letters are effective, because he himself strove to live in attentiveness of God's love and presence in his own daily life. Marmion is referred to as the "Doctor of Divine Adoption." He emphasized that Christians are truly adopted children of God through baptism and are thus to abandon themselves into the loving hands of the Father at all times. To entrust oneself to the Father and model oneself on the life of Christ was everything to Dom Marmion.

Abbot Marmion's writings were a staple of spirituality in the twentieth century for the generation preceding the Second Vatican Council. Recently, a resurgence of interest has been occurring, which recognizes that this master of spirituality has something profound to offer Christians today in the twenty-first century. He was dedicated to writing to his spiritual children and encouraging them in their struggles to keep moving forward on their journey of faith. He helped countless men and women draw ever closer to Christ.

It is well documented by classmates of Karol Woytyla, the future Pope John Paul II, that he was an avid reader of Marmion's writings. Columba Marmion was beatified during the Jubilee Year 2000. In the homily at the beatification, Pope John Paul II stated: "May a widespread rediscovery of the spiritual writings of Blessed Columba Marmion help priests, religious and laity to grow in union with Christ and bear faithful witness to him through ardent love of God and generous service of their brothers and sisters." This recognition by the Church Universal reveals not only Marmion's personal sanctity, but also the profundity of his writings.

Blessed Teresa of Calcutta considered *Union with God* to be her favorite work from which she drew great solace. It should be no surprise that Marmion's teaching of childlike trust in Divine Providence and abandonment to the will of the Father would find in Mother Teresa such a devotee. The entire order of the Missionaries of Charity continues to draw inspiration from Marmion's works. Mother Teresa would quote from him extensively, even citing him in her original hand-written copy of the *Constitutions of the Missionaries of Charity*. In an early letter to her sisters dated 1961, she paraphrases Marmion: "Fidelity to the rule is the most precious and delicate flower of love we religious can offer to Almighty God." In 1967 she wrote: "In reading Dom Marmion I find in him so much of what our Society expects of us, Holiness!" Marmion's theme of joyfully persevering in the midst of struggles was Mother Teresa's attitude for the order which she founded and to which she herself subscribed.

Marmion's uncomplicated yet insightful wisdom, as found in the pages of this book, should be a gift for many in today's seemingly complicated world. His very readable presentation of the gospel truths for everyday life is as relevant now as when it was first written. This work will edify all readers to be more faithful to Christ, to His Church, and to their vocation in life. There is encouragement in these pages to live as children of our loving Father and to be ever more faithful to Him in both the simple and the profound moments of life. The whole of the Christian life is to be one of union with God. The key for Dom Marmion was abandonment to the will of the Father in all things, doing all for the love of God.

St. Vincent de Paul Regional Seminary
Boynton Beach, Florida
Holy Thursday 2006

INTRODUCTION
to the original edition, by
Archbishop Goodier, S.J.

My dear Reverend Father,

I am deeply grateful for the privilege you offer me in asking me to introduce this edition of the letters of Dom Columba Marmion to its future readers. You speak of me in the beautiful life you have written as one of his intimate friends.[1] Yes, in one sense I may have had that honor; and yet it is true that I never actually spoke to him or met him. Our friendship, if it may be given that name, began in this way. Once, when I was still in India, I received a most personal letter, as from one who had known me all my life, and signed, "Dom Columba Marmion." The writer said he had read something I had published, and that he knew from it that we were "kindred souls." He asked, in consequence, that we should write to one another, and so come to know one another, sharing each other's spiritual experiences for our mutual benefit.

Such a letter, spontaneous, obviously genuine in every word, naturally took me by surprise; I doubt whether I was ever more surprised by any letter I have received in all my life. I had often heard of Dom Columba; I had crossed his path many times, in giving retreats in England where he had been before me; I had heard many echoes of the beautiful things he taught, and had sometimes wished that I might meet him. But when sent to India at the beginning of the war I gave up all hope or idea of such a thing; I had to bid goodbye to old associations, and to many old friends, I could not think of meeting new ones in Europe. Hence my astonishment at receiving this first letter from Dom Columba, as trustful, as intimate, as if we had known one another from childhood.

But you will understand me when I say that his spontaneity quite captured me; above all, you, who have lived with him many years, and have shown us in the Life how this simplicity and frankness explain Dom Columba's fascination. At once I found myself writing back to him in the same spirit. One who had, as it seemed, revealed to me his whole self in the first letter he wrote to me, could not but win from me a revelation of myself to him. I wrote, imitating, as well as I could, his simple manner; I compared my life in India with his in Maredsous; I tried to let him see myself in my surrounding, warning him that those surroundings were not such as would be likely to cultivate the life of contemplation.

This was the beginning of our correspondence and our friendship. Almost immediately he wrote again, taking my letter and commenting upon it, not contrasting but comparing my life with his own, and showing the love of God, and the hand of God, in both. In this second letter again, he let me look into the depths of his soul, as if it could not occur to him to do otherwise. Moreover, another proof of that simplicity, combined with human affection, which was behind all else, with this letter he sent me his photograph; as much as to say that if we were never to meet in the flesh, at least I should know what manner of man he was, outside as well as within. So our correspondence began, and it continued. Once, when on account of a long visitation, I had allowed an interval to come between one of his letters and my reply, he wrote again chiding me for my silence; and once more it was the same beautiful and simple story, the revealing of God as he found Him within his soul and his own life.

My last letter was answered by another hand; if I am not mistaken, it was your own. I had written as usual, telling him a little more of our mission as well as of myself, and even asking whether there were any Benedictines at Maredsous whom he could send out to help me; for by that time, owing to the scarcity after the war, I had received permission from Rome to get missionaries from whatever source I could. But long before my request reached Maredsous he had gone to heaven. I read the news first in a paper, then in a letter from a friend; I need not say what a shock it gave me. Our friendship had ended as suddenly as it had begun; it had passed like a very gleaming meteor through a very dark sky.

As I read your selection from his letters, and your comments on them and their author, I cannot help feeling that you, too, must have been to him, even more than myself, a "kindred soul." For, in the first place, you have called attention to that in Dom Columba Marmion which seems to me his most striking trait; he wrote, not merely from the knowledge he had gained from study, he wrote always from the experience of his own soul. He described God to others as he knew Him within himself; when he spoke of union with God, its elements and its conditions, all unconsciously, because so spontaneously, he revealed the course, and the development, and the perfection of his own spiritual life. That is surely one of the secrets of the influence of his books on so many, belonging to various nationalities and schools, lay people as well as religious. They know they are reading the teaching, not of a master but of one who himself has toiled and labored, not as one above them but as one of themselves.

And a second characteristic of Dom Columba followed from this. He saw the bright side of every one and of every thing, he would not allow it to be dimmed. A soul might be depressed, but he would not leave it in depression; troubles, might come from outside, but he would always see in them the hand of God. Even sin he treated in a way quite his own. He would not delay over it, there were other things far more important to think about: when it comes, let us get rid of it as soon as possible, he seemed to say, and push on to something better. Here his natural simplicity helped him, and helped others, with a kind of reassuring insight. Dom Columba had no use for sin in his own straight, beautiful life, and he would not have others linger over it, not even by excessive lamentation, or by excessive fear. If they would lament, let them weep over the sufferings of Jesus and leave themselves alone; if they would fear, let it be the fear of a loving child for a loving Father, not the fear of a mere offender and no more.

These, it seems to me, were the two gifts possessed by Dom Columba, which have found for him access into the hearts of so many. You show very admirably how they lead at once to the extremes of perfection. Other, more systematic writers, give Union with God as the climax of the spiritual life; it is usually given, and quite rightly, as the last chapter of spiritual books. Still, in describing the spirituality of Dom Columba, you have felt that you must place it, not last but first; and not only first, but dominating all the rest. Union with God is the one goal of all desire; therefore Dom Columba would set it before the souls he guided from the very beginning. He would tell them in what it consisted, how it was to be recognized and proved, by what steps it was to be attained. He would show how it gave a color to every other feature of the soul, its desires, its renunciation, its virtues. In the very order in which you have set your study of Dom Columba in his letters, it seems to me that you have brought out very well the sum and the crown of his teaching.

I do not think I need say any more. Those who know Dom Columba from his other works will find him here putting into practice, for himself and for others, the lessons he has taught elsewhere. On that account this book may be of even more use to many souls than what they have read before. In these letters they will find answers to their own questions, practical guidance in the course they should follow, simple regulations for ordinary lives even while the highest ideals are never suffered to pass out of sight. Your book will increase the influence of Dom Columba Marmion among countless followers, both in the world and in the cloister; and that is the reward which, I am sure, is all you look for after much toil, carried on, obviously, with much love.

I wish you every blessing.

> St. Scholastica's Abbey
> Teignmouth, South Devon
> September 14, 1933

PREFACE

to the original edition, by
Dom Raymond Thibaut

IN STUDYING Dom Marmion as a letter-writer, we have elsewhere analyzed at length the many qualities which made him an eminent spiritual director.[2] "He comes before us," we were able to conclude, "in the simple light of a very high and very humble human personality, and also in the splendor of that close union with God which was the secret of his fervent and enlightened zeal for souls. We see him a ready and responsive instrument in his Lord's hands, remaining near to us by his radiant goodness, and ever widening hearts by uplifting them towards the summits."[3]

The reader will again find all these qualities in the present work. We may however be allowed to indicate a few of its characteristic points.

Dom Marmion's spiritual letters constitute above all a doctrinal treasure. Direction, as he understands and practices it, is a work of light. He lights up the path of perfection before enlisting souls to walk in it. Darkness and error are the first obstacles to be dispersed. Can one walk quickly in the night? What good is it to run on any but the right track? Christ asked His Father to sanctify His disciples in the truth (John 17:17).

Dom Marmion never forgets this. By turn of mind, by inmost conviction, he always makes his practical conclusions flow from the light of his principles.[4] It is in the "deifying light"[5] that this master of spirituality seeks for the lights wherewith he wishes to inundate the souls that come to him. As he loves to say, God alone being the Author of holiness, can alone, according to His good pleasure, show the way of holiness: "We must seek God as God wishes us to seek Him, otherwise we shall not find Him."

For in the guidance of souls Dom Marmion is always intent on discovering what are God's views for them, and careful to lead them gently to the most perfect and loving submission to God's good pleasure: a tendency which contributes to imprint a deeply supernatural character on his work of direction, and to ensure for it an eminent influence for good.

However, in this correspondence there is nothing of the theorist or lecturer.

The teaching that this doctor of the spiritual life gives us, he has first of all assimilated; he has made it his own, and has but to let his pen run on: he writes from the abundance of his heart and experience. Now, with strong swift upward flight, he draws the soul up to the summits, then, in more familiar guise, he makes her walk in the valley, embellishing his points, exhortations, and counsels, here and there, with a touch of humor, a witty remark, an apt illustration. Most often, he writes "simply, without either art or color, for these matters have no need of them, simplicity being their beauty as it is that of God, their Author."[6]

Always very supernatural, Dom Marmion is, at the same time very human; with him "the most comprehensive and gentlest charity softens and transforms the austere demands of perfection into appeals full of confidence."[7]

Even when he shows himself insistent, this master of asceticism does not, however, lose his affectionate fatherly manner, and the kindly tone which finds its way into all hearts. We can apply to him what has been very truly written concerning one of the most winning of spiritual directors, Saint Anselm: "He speaks to each soul the language she is able to understand, delicately taking her at the propitious moment when she is most favorably disposed. Thus, disdaining no mode of approach, he gains and fathoms the soul to make her understand the divine will for her in particular, and having won her, makes her finally docile to grace and to the Holy Spirit: and often the victories of his kindness and gentleness are those of a very exacting divine love."[8]

We may add that Dom Marmion's correspondents are to be met with in every state of life. Doubtless, many of his letters are to persons living in the religious state, but we know that in the eyes of this master of spirituality "the religious state, taken in what is essential, does not constitute a particular form of existence on the borders, or at the side of Christianity, it is this same Christianity lived in its fullness in the pure light of the Gospel."[9] Hence, in his teachings to the privileged souls of the cloister, we shall see him insist, before all things, on the very principles which govern all Christ's disciples: A simple Christian in the world could, without difficulty and with good result, appropriate to himself the life-giving substance of the doctrine that he sets before them.[10]

The present publication of letters is not integral; it could not be so, many letters not having been sent to us, and on the other hand, several of Dom Marmion's correspondents being still living.[11]

Must these letters still be left buried away for long years, until the time comes when we shall be able to bring out a complete edition of them? Or would it not be to the great advantage of souls to give them the benefit now, in the largest measure possible, of these spiritual treasures? It is upon this second opinion

that we have thought it right to fix our choice; and, in agreement
with the persons to whom these letters were addressed, and
whose confidence honors, as much as it touches us, we have
decided not to delay longer before offering this volume to the
public.[12]

The fragmentary character of the publication obliged us—as
likewise the doctrinal nature of the letters allowed—to adopt a
logical order of arrangement. Our plan has been inspired by the
central idea which predominates in all these letters—namely,
that of union of the soul with God. The general conception of
this union, its diverse constitutive elements, the conditions of its
progress, its expansion: such are the leading thoughts around
which we have grouped, in as natural an order as possible, the
numerous extracts selected: in this way the different chapters of
this work have taken form. It may then be regarded in a certain
manner like a small treatise on the life of union with God envis-
aged under its most essential aspects. A glance at the Table of
Contents will show the simplicity of the plan, and its logical
arrangement.[13]

We are confident that these pages will meet with a favorable
reception from the many friends of *Christ, the Life of the Soul*.
They will find again the same doctrine, high and accessible,
supernatural and human, under a more familiar form, but not
less well-balanced. We are sure that the reading of this book
will have a great influence for good. At the same time as further
revealing the abundance of light with which God inundated
Dom Marmion's soul, it will extend the spiritual radiance of an
admirable doctrine of life.

Abbey of Maredsous
Feast of the Dedication of the Basilica of St. Benedict
August 19, 1933

TRANSLATOR'S NOTE

A CERTAIN NUMBER of these letters of Dom Marmion were written in English; these extracts are marked with an asterisk * at the beginning of the citation.

It was Dom Marmion's custom to underline certain words in order to give emphasis to his thought or to draw special attention to it; we have respected this custom by printing in *italics* the words he underlined once, and in SMALL CAPITALS the words he underlined twice.

It may be here observed that, in whichever language he speaks or writes, Dom Marmion uses the French word *abandon* in the sense of self-abandonment or self-surrender.

Finally, the extracts from his letters have been published only with the assent of those to whom they were addressed, but more than once, through discretion, we have not given the date.

Union with God

CHAPTER I

UNION WITH GOD:
GENERAL IDEA

The following passage appears to us to be well calculated to give the essence of Dom Marmion's conception of the subject of union with God.[14] This conception is assuredly none other than that of the Gospel, of Saint Paul and of Saint John, but he has condensed it in precise and luminous terms.

Holiness, in man, is only possible according to the Divine Plan: to know this plan, to adapt oneself to it, is the whole substance of holiness.

This plan consists in calling the human creature to participate, by the grace of supernatural adoption, in God's own eternal life.

At the center of this plan is established Christ, the God-Man, in whom dwells the fullness of Divine life, the life which He comes to communicate to mankind.

Man enters into participation of this Divine life by sanctifying grace, which, while leaving him in his condition of creature, makes him truly, by adoption, the child of God: the Heavenly Father encompasses all Christians in an extension of His Fatherhood in relation to His own Son Jesus Christ.

This grace of adoption, transcending, as it does, the rights, powers, and strict requirements of our nature, has therefore an essentially supernatural character. While keeping its nature in what is noble and good, the soul has to strive to live as a child of God, under the action of the Holy Spirit.

In consequence of these fundamental doctrines, Dom Marmion required of the soul he directed a twofold essential attitude: the humble submission of the creature and the loving faithfulness of the child.

He would have the soul, conscious of the rights of God, acknowledge these rights, and honor and respect them by perfect conformity of the will with that of Jesus. But being the child of the Heavenly Father, all this work of conformity must be rooted in constant filial love. Dom Marmion unceasingly invited the soul to come and ever to keep in contact with God by looking upon Him in faith, turning towards Him in confidence and in impelling love. On every occasion to lift up the soul to God, the one Fount of life and a Father full of loving-kindness, and to draw immediately from this ever living and ever accessible source the light that illumines, the strength whereby temptation is resisted, obstacles are overcome, victory is won over self, sacrifices are accepted, humiliations welcomed, trials received and, finally, the duty of the present moment is fulfilled.

And all this through Jesus Christ, the one and only way that leads to the Father, by having recourse to His merits; by constant union with the interior dispositions of the Incarnate Word, the God-Man, the living Model of all perfection, and by the action of His Spirit, the Author of all holiness.

Dom Marmion would have the soul endeavor to steep its whole life and activity, even to the smallest details, in the supernatural, and to learn from a lively faith, a confident, filial, humble and generous love, the secret of all progress.

We shall need to recall these ideas in order to grasp the value of the quotations we are about to give.

In a letter[15] so remarkable for its clearness that for this reason it must be placed at the very outset of this book, Dom Marmion throws a light on the three spirits which dispute the empire over souls, he characterizes their action and lays down a general rule for discerning them:

In every soul three spirits strive for the mastery. The spirit of falsehood and blasphemy who from the beginning ever suggests the exact contrary of what God whispers. "If you eat of this fruit you shall certainly die," said God. "You shall not die by any means"[16] was Satan's reply, and all his suggestions are but the echo of this first lie.

Then there is the spirit of this world, inclining us to judge things according to the maxims of sense and of carnal prudence. "The prudence of this world is folly with God."

Then there is the spirit of God ever whispering in our ears to raise our hearts above nature: *Sursum corda,* lift up your hearts. To live by faith: "My just man liveth by faith."[17] This Spirit always inclines us towards simple loving faith, abandon of self into God's hands. It fills us with "peace and joy in believing," and produces the fruits of which Saint Paul speaks.

Now, my dear child, in certain persons the action of these several spirits is more tangible and striking than in others. In you the influence of these spirits is very marked. You will always know them by their fruits, even though Satan may try to clothe himself as an angel of light. Our Lord says, You will recognize these spirits by the *fruits* they produce in your soul.[18]

God's Spirit, even when He reproaches us or inclines us to confusion or compunction for our sins, *ever* fills the soul with peace and filial confidence in our Heavenly Father. The other spirits dry up our soul, fill us with naturalistic tendencies, or, if it be the spirit of hell, casts gloom and discouragement into our soul. Now just as Eve *should* have refused to believe or even to listen to the infernal spirit, when he contradicted God's testimony, just as she ought to have put him to flight by saying like Saint Michael, "Who is like unto God?[19] Do you think I will pay attention to your hissing lies, when they contradict God's word?" So should we.

I recommend you a great fidelity to the movements of the Holy Spirit. Your baptism and your confirmation have established Him as a living fountain in your soul. Hear His whisperings, and put the other inspirations to flight *at once.* If you are faithful in this, little by little this Divine Spirit will become your guide and bear you with Him into God's bosom. The Holy Spirit holds the place for us that Jesus did for His apostles during His mortal life. Just as they could have recourse to Him, speak to Him, pray, etc., so He has sent us "Another Paraclete to stay with us and teach us all things which He has told us."[20]

A few weeks before his death,[21] Dom Marmion traced in two vigorous clauses the general line of God's thought concerning us:

I can say with Saint John that I have no greater joy than to see my children walking in the truth.[22] To be in the truth, we must be in the Word, for He is the Truth. "I am Truth."[23]

Now, the truth supposes that we live and act according to the relations which God has established for our nature and our dignity as children of God.

1. Our nature supposes that the *creature* remain always in most humble adoration before the Creator: that is so essential that *nothing* can change it. Our adoption to the state of child of God raises our nature, but does not destroy it. Hence it comes that when we rebel against God's will, against His permissions, we are no longer in the true attitude of the creature.

2. Our adoption as *children* supposes that we act always as loving children towards our Heavenly Father, constantly

seeking His good pleasure: "Seek His Face evermore."[24] This *Facies Dei,* Face of God, is the smile of His loving approbation. If you always keep the truth of this twofold relation, you will be more and more fixed in truth and in peace.

Sometimes, according to the state of the soul in question, Dom Marmion draws attention to only one of these two aspects, namely our condition as creature. To a contemplative nun he recalls the necessity of adoration and compunction:

In the way of direction this is what I think useful to say to you:

1. Be very true with God, and as soon as you let yourself be drawn away to any fault or unfaithfulness (which will happen from time to time) look your Heavenly Father in the face, and show Him your soul in the bare truth.

2. Never lay holy compunction entirely aside; it is the most humble expression of the forgiven prodigal child, but which says with David: "My sin is ALWAYS before me."[25] The prayer which Saint Teresa wrote and kept upon her prie-dieu was: "Enter not into judgment with Thy servant,"[26] and however high her contemplation might be, this humble compunction always remained in the depth of her heart. Saint Catherine of Siena on coming out of her ecstasies used to say: "I have sinned, Lord, have mercy on me." A soul which keeps holy compunction will never go astray.

3. However intimate may be the union to which Our Lord admits you, do not forget that He is God, the Infinite! The love of the creature, in order to be true, must be the love of adoration; the Sacred Humanity of Jesus stands before the face of the Father in the reverence of infinite love: "He shall be FILLED with the spirit of the fear of the Lord."[27]

If you follow the counsels of your father, there is no danger.[28]

In another circumstance, we see him rather encouraging a timorous person, but one of good will, to filial confidence, the condition of liberty of spirit:

* I am very *glad indeed* you were inspired to take up Saint Gertrude. Her spirit is just the antidote for your spiritual ills. Her view of our faults is absolutely true. Faults arising from weakness and really detested in our hearts do not prevent God from loving us. They excite His compassion: "As a father hath compassion on his children, so hath the Lord compassion on them that fear Him, FOR HE KNOWS HOW WE ARE FORMED."[29] This was Saint Paul's great devotion, to present himself before his Heavenly Father with all his infirmities, and as he looked on himself always as a member of Jesus Christ, these infirmities were really Christ's. "Gladly therefore will I glory in my infirmities, that the power of Christ may dwell in me."[30] Try and fill yourself with that spirit of childlike confidence in God.

It appears to me that the more closely I become united with our Divine Lord, the more He draws me towards His Father, the more He wills me to be filled with His filial spirit.

You could not do better than follow out that thought. It is the whole spirit of the New Law: "For you have not received the spirit of bondage again in fear; but you have received the spirit of ADOPTION of sons, whereby we cry: 'Abba, Father!'"[31]

Most of your difficulties come from your not allowing yourself to be guided and inspired by this spirit of love, but listen too often to the other spirit of fear, which paralyzes your soul and prevents God's grace.[32]

It is to this thought of filial submission that he returns most often in his letters, namely, that the substance of the whole life of union

---

* Passages with an asterisk were written by Dom Marmion in English.

lies in the fulfillment, out of love, of the Heavenly Father's will in
union with the dispositions of Jesus Christ:

Perfection lies in accomplishing God's will, out of love. At
the moment of the Incarnation, the first movement of the Holy
Humanity of Jesus, that movement which according to the
saying of Saint Paul summed up *all holiness,* was the acceptance
of the Divine Will: "At the head of the book, it is written of me
that I should do Thy will... Behold I come to do Thy will, O
God." And Mary's whole life is contained in these words,
"Behold the handmaid of the Lord, be it done to me according
to Thy word."[33]

**Dom Marmion feared nothing so much as to see a soul labor under an
illusion on this subject. On this point his solicitude is especially keen
and he frequently gave expression to it. Passages abound which
testify to the great care he took to make souls live in the truth:**

I pray for you with all my heart that Our Lord may hold you
by the hand and make you know and do His holy will.[34]

Let things evolve under God's hand, and once come to "the
point" we shall see more clearly what has to be done. For the
moment I don't see distinctly what is the Divine will. In a complicated situation the only resource is *oculus simplex,* a simple
eye. If, in everything, you look solely at God, putting personal
considerations aside, "having no part of darkness,"[35] you will be
in light and peace.[36]

I am so happy to see that in the midst of so *much* business you
keep your eyes fixed on God. "CONSIDER THE END"—that will
keep you in the truth—"and all that you do shall prosper."[37]

I am praying *continually* that God may keep you very close to
His Heart *in the truth* and that the enemy may not succeed in the
midst of the fogs of the moment in detaching you from the
Divine will, that is to say from God Himself.[38]

And again, a few days later:

Keep your eye well fixed on the light and let no dust enter into it. Try as far as possible to keep your soul exposed to the Divine rays, for apart from that, light is nothing but darkness.[39]

If you keep the eye of your soul fixed upon God alone, you will receive many graces.[40]

To the mother of a family:

I pray for you with all my heart that God may give you the grace and light to accomplish His holy will perfectly in the hard task He lays upon you of bringing up such a large family for Him.[41]

Some souls—often generous ones—at times let themselves be attracted by the mirage of an apparently higher good but which does not enter into God's views for them. Dom Marmion puts them on their guard against such a dangerous illusion:

If circumstances happen to change, *then and not before,* we can consider how you would have to adapt your life to the new position that you set before me. For the moment, live *in the actual present,* and not in a future which perhaps will never be an actuality for you.[42]

Indeed the union of our will with that of God is the only fruitful source; a multitude of variations exist on this theme. We have but to thread a few notes together:

The most brilliant actions, those that attract the attention and praise of all the world, are only worth anything in God's sight in as far as they are "made in God," that is to say in entire dependence upon Him and done for love of Him. When one is really united with God and, consequently, in the light of His truth, one sees things differently than people in the world.[43]

I rejoice to see that in every circumstance you consider the end, namely, God alone, and that therefore you see these circumstances in their true light. God Who is "the Beginning"[44] wills to take the initiative in the direction of your life; we shall fail in our end and object if we lay claim to substitute our views for those of God. This is above all true of those who have made religious profession.[45]

I was thinking much about you yesterday [date of his correspondent's feast] and I prayed Our Lord to take you all to Himself, for I see more and more every day that apart from God all is vanity, and that in Him all becomes divine.[46]

You ought to remit yourself into the hands of the good God, our Heavenly Father. He loves you more and far better than you could ever love yourself. You will only do *what is really good* where God is with you. "I will be with thee."[47]

And this, in truly "Columbanian" style:

Let yourself be led by God's Hand without looking too much where He is leading you, provided that you remain quite submissive and in His Hands. One is a thousand times more united to God in the midst of a crowd where one is by obedience than hidden away in one's cell by self-love.[48]

The source of supernatural fruitfulness, this union with the Divine will is likewise the principle of deep peace. The following citation is taken from one of Dom Marmion's earliest letters of direction, May 21, 1895. We already find him just as he is, fully supernatural and intensely human:

I very much wish that you could acquire calm and peace, and it is certainly an inspiration of the Holy Spirit that is urging you in this direction. Only do it *very gently and quietly* and don't be too much distressed if you don't succeed straight away. The best means of acquiring this calm is an *absolute* resignation to God's holy will, there you will find the region of peace and...[49] Try to wish for nothing, to attach your heart to nothing without having first presented it to God and placed it in the Sacred Heart, in order to wish it *in Him* and *with Him*.

One of the chief reasons why we lose peace of soul is that we desire something, our heart clings to some object, without knowing if God wills it or not, and then, when an obstacle is opposed to our desires, we are troubled, we are no longer in conformity with His holy will, and we lose peace.

However, know that grace does not destroy nature, but sanctifies it, and that everyone must take their character into account. So, in trying to avoid too great eagerness, take the just measure, for with your lively character to act too slowly would be an affectation which I want you to avoid at any cost.

CHAPTER II

Union with God:

Its Elements

1. *Love: Principle of Union*

The principle of this union with God is only to be found in love. We here touch upon one of the characteristic points of Dom Marmion's doctrine. From the year 1887 Dom Marmion had been in possession of this doctrine[50] which throughout his life he so ably and happily put into practice. His continuity of thought on this point is remarkable; with him it is a thought which takes every form and shape; he repeats it to all whatever may be their particular state of life, for the precept of charity is universal and if he does not always write it, like Saint Francis de Sales, "in large hand,"[51] he frequently underlines it.

To a very young girl living in the world:

Try to do *all* for love of Jesus; He is so good that He accepts the least thing, provided that it is done out of love.[52]

And again some ten years later:

Try, my dear child, to do *all for love.* God is Love, and He accepts the least things done for love's sake. Love is like the philosopher's stone which turns all that it touches into gold.[53]

The same to a contemplative religious:

Try, my dear daughter, to do each action with great love, and

13

in the name—not of Helen [her name before she entered the religious life]—but in the name of Jesus... God bless you and make you *all His own.*[54]

It is what Saint Paul himself says, "whether you eat or drink, or whatsoever else you do, do all to the glory of God." Divine love takes possession of all in order to ennoble all and make it pleasing to God. And nothing is more consoling for those who seek God in uprightness of heart and simplicity of humility.

Dom Marmion seized the smallest occasion to recall this valuable principle. Here we have him replying at the beginning of the year to one of his young student monks:

Thank you for your little word. You know, without my needing to tell you so, how much I am ever united with you in the love of Our Lord. No need to offer you my good wishes, since I bear you every day to the holy altar. This year will be a fatiguing and distracting one for you, but done in obedience and for love, "all things work together unto good."[55]

Let us try to love Our dear Savior with *all* our heart, for all is in that. The days, months and years succeed one another, and nothing remains but God and what we do for Him.[56]

He writes to another:

I congratulate you on your success and on the merits you have gained in applying yourself to studies that are wearisome to you. If your studies done in obedience and for love of God secure you the privilege of finding yourself more deeply in Him for all eternity, certainly it is not time lost.[57]

To a nun, his exhortation becomes urgent:

* Jesus is longing for your love; once for all give Him your *whole* heart and your *whole* love. This love is a gift which comes from Him, and it is in Communion that He gives it.[58]

To exhortation he joins prayer:

I will indeed pray for you on your feast day, that God may take you into His arms, or rather into His Heart, and that He will accomplish in you all His good pleasure.[59]

It is a joy to his apostolic heart to notice the progress of a soul on this royal high road. He writes to a young girl:

I am so glad that you are following the counsel I gave you to offer each action to Jesus out of love. Saint Magdalen de Pazzi says that when one acts solely for God, our whole life becomes a continual act of divine love and that we advance very quickly in holiness.[60]

And to a nun, these profound words:

Having left all for love, your whole life is a prayer, for one prays in the innermost soul without knowing it as long as one remains faithfully in the track laid down by the Divine Will. Try, without over fatiguing your head to multiply acts of love; they uplift the whole life and give it fresh value. That is the true way to acquire the *Christian* virtues. The natural virtues can be acquired by our own efforts, examens of conscience, etc. But the Christian virtues, which are an emanation from the virtues of Christ, come only from Him. "And of His fullness we have all received."[61]

In the same strain, these lines, expressing an identical thought, convey the echo of his own sentiments a few months before his death:

* I am so glad you are going to God in *His way,* that is by:
1. Perfect *abandon* of yourself and all your interests to His love;
2. By the conscientious discharge of duty for His love;
3. By patience and silence.[62]

We find happy and telling developments of this doctrine in many of these letters. Here in very simple language Dom Marmion explains it to a lovable child not yet fifteen years old:

You know that when we are in a state of grace, Jesus abides *always* in our heart. His great desire is to be *all* for us. It seems like a dream too beautiful to be true that Jesus so good, so powerful, so tender, wishes to be our Brother, and yet it is He Himself Who says so. "Whosoever shall do the will of My Father, that is in heaven, he is My brother, and sister, and mother."[63] These are Jesus' very own words. So to arrive at the happiness of having Jesus as our Brother, our closest Friend, we must do His Father's will.

Well! what is His will?

First of all, to avoid sin, and if we fall into it by frailty to ask forgiveness at once.

Next, to do all our actions for Him. For you, that is easy. Your "order of the day" is fixed; you know your duties; it only remains to sanctify them by consecrating them to God.[64]

What he explains to a child, he repeats twenty years later to a contemplative nun:

The value of our whole life depends on the motive by which we act.[65] Now it is certain that the highest motive is that of love. Saint Paul said, "Who loved me, and delivered Himself for me."[66] This conviction of the love of Christ constrained the apostle to give himself all to Christ. His answer was, "I most gladly will spend and be spent myself."[67] Once a soul has thus given herself out of love, nothing stays her, neither sufferings, nor difficulties, nor all that troubles us, for "where love is, labor is absent."[68] Try then to give yourself to Christ in this way without reserve, "for good" and out of love. Then all will go on well. Your life will be extremely pleasing to God and very meritorious.[69]

Let us read these lines, so clear and decisive, so much too in his own manner and spirit:

The surest, the shortest, the most luminous way, also the sweetest, is the way of love. If anyone love Me, says Jesus, "I will manifest Myself to him." My dear child, you are a little like a volcano; there are still many scoriae [cinders] in you but there is also fire, and what you need is to walk in this way of love. You ought not to seek any other remedy. But to walk in this way needs great fidelity.

Do all things solely for love of Our Lord and, for love of Him, accept all that He permits; give yourself up to love without looking either to the right or the left. Accept, without troubling yourself about them, the annoyances and difficulties through which you are passing at present. What you have to do by obedience, do as well as ever you can, but without being anxious whether others are pleased with you or blame you, whether they love you or don't love you. It ought to be enough for you to be loved by Our Lord.

Have but one thing in view, namely to love Our Lord and to please Him in everything. If you walk in this way of love, you will see in three or four weeks what a change will take place in your soul; you will know how to pray, God will draw near to you, He will abide in you, you will live in the fellowship of the Father, the Son and the Holy Spirit.

And say often to God, "My God, You indeed merit that I love You solely and that I seek but You."[70]

And again, to the same correspondent:

Seek in all things to give pleasure to Our Lord; do all with a great purity of intention. Before each action, say to Our Lord, "My Jesus, I wish to do this solely for love of You; and if this action did not please You, I would not do it." If we do everything solely for love of Christ it is impossible for Him to fail to unite Himself to us. "The Father hath not left Me alone, for I do always the things that please Him."[71] It is the same for us: Our Lord will keep us ever united to Himself if we do all things with the sole intention of pleasing Him.[72]

On this point, Dom Marmion shows the necessity of carefully controlling the movements of the soul. To a young girl:

When you write, tell me:

1. If you are often united with Our Lord during the day;

2. If you are faithful to form a very pure intention before each action of any importance;

3. If you habitually follow your first movements or if you are beginning to practice interior mortification in repressing from time to time the vivacity of your character in order that Our Lord may become the only Master of your soul.[73]

At about the same period he traces out this program admirable in its psychology:

Examine yourself on the following points.

1. Examine thoroughly the *intention* with which you act. The love with which you act is a *thousand* times more important than the *material exactitude* of your actions.

2. Examine the question as to whether your heart is wholly free: *a*) as regards persons; *b*) as regards occupations, being ready at any moment to change your occupation at the least sign of the Divine Will; *c*) as regards things, holding to nothing, neither for yourself nor for others, if charity so demands.

3. God ALONE is necessary for you. You will find all in Him. Hold fast to nothing but Him. But,

4. Yield yourself up without reserve to Him and to all that He loves.

Circumstances oblige a young girl to defer her entry into religion; these are the practical counsels she should follow:

I recommend you:

1. To aim at great purity of intention in all that you do. Let Jesus be the *eye of your soul*,[74] that is to say, try to unite yourself to Him in all His intentions, so that He may bear you Himself towards His Father. Your actions in God's sight are worth: *a)* the intention from which they proceed; *b)* the zeal with which you perform them for Him.

2. Continue to communicate as in the past. That is your strength, the source of your divine life. "As the living Father hath sent Me, and *I live* by the Father; so he that eateth Me, the same also shall *live* for and by Me."

3. Shun every relationship that could turn you away from your end and aim.

4. As far as possible, never omit *a little* spiritual reading.

5. Immolate nature to grace in everything.[75]

More than twenty years later he discovers the austere and wide vistas of love to one who had just crossed the threshold of the cloister:

* When I met you during the retreat, I *saw* that beneath your wild girlish nature, there was a very deep sanctuary capable of great love; and I know that Jesus wants that *all* for Himself. You understand this too, and the program of the spiritual life which you propose in your letter is *just* what the Holy Ghost wants of you.

1. Do *all* through love.

2. For love, work, suffer, bear up despite monotony, just as Jesus on the cross.

3. If He asks for anything, never refuse, but if it seems too hard to nature, pray, pray till He gives you the grace.

4. Keep the eye of your soul fixed on your *one* Love for Whom you have left all. If anything comes between you and Him, He will show it to you in the light of His Face.

What I told you: "He wants you to do all for love," came directly from His Heart. Pray for me daily as I shall for you. May God bless and love you, and make you a holocaust of love united with your Crucified Spouse.[76]

In the evening of his life, he summed up his teaching on this point in a sentence comprising the whole secret of that perfection which he himself had sought:

* Try to *smile lovingly* at every manifestation of God's will.

Such a doctrine so constantly preached and above all so fully lived enabled Dom Marmion to understand the secret of the little way of love of Sister Thérèse of the Child Jesus.

On being begged in January 1911—we shall notice the date—to add his contribution to the request for the Cause of the Servant of God to be introduced at Rome, he wrote to the Sovereign Pontiff the following lines of which we have had the good fortune to find the original.[77]

In our day, these lines will appear almost commonplace, now that so much has been written to familiarize us with the spirit of the Saint of Lisieux. At the period when they were written they show a singular justness of insight; with rare precision Dom Marmion specified, in a few essential points according to his custom, the teaching to be deduced from the life of the holy Carmelite, and her providential mission. These lines form the happy and quite natural complement of the doctrine set before us in this chapter.

Most Holy Father, God Who is admirable in all His works, and above all in His Saints, chooses His elect out of every class of society and among persons of very different character and temperament. He thus aids our weakness by showing us that heroic sanctity is not the exclusive privilege of those of a certain vocation and special temperament, but that the invitation, "Be ye therefore perfect, as also your Heavenly Father is perfect,"[78] is addressed to all.

It seems that in this age when few feel called to go to God by the career of the sublime austerities of former times, God wills to show us that love can supply for everything, and that this way of love is the easiest and shortest way of perfection.

Sister Thérèse of the Holy Child Jesus, Carmelite of the Carmel of Lisieux, appears to us to be a shining confirmation of this truth. She said of herself that in Christ's Mystical Body she desired to be the heart and to do all through love. And this love, mother of every virtue, was expressed in her by that perfect fidelity to all her duties, by that absolute abandon to God's good pleasure, by that boundless confidence in the goodness and love of her Heavenly Father, which are the perfect expression of the Spirit of Adoption.

Most Holy Father, we believe that in placing Sister Thérèse of the Child of Jesus upon our altars, Your Holiness will be presenting to the world a model of that perfection, the fruit of the infinite mercy of the Sacred Heart, which is the best adapted to the weakness of human nature in our days.

Therefore I most humbly implore Your Holiness graciously to ordain the procedure relative to the cause of this Servant of God for the greatest glory of God and for the edification of the Church.

Humbly prostrate at the feet of Your Holiness, I beg with confidence the Apostolic Benediction.

2. *Fidelity: Proof of Love*

Under penalty of being but a phantom or illusion, love must be manifested in deeds of which it is the principle, and this love must generously shape the course of the soul's whole activity. Recalling the words of Jesus, "If you love Me, keep My commandments," Dom Marmion wrote, "Fidelity is the one touchstone of real love."[79] Reference to this main principle is often to be met with in his spiritual works; we find it again, not less explicit nor less frequent, in his correspondence:

To be intimately united to God, it is necessary:

1. To make a habit of doing everything to please God. If one strives, out of love, at every moment, to please God, after a certain time, God gives Himself and one lives continually with Him in faith.

2. Great fidelity, because God is a jealous God, He does not unite Himself to an unfaithful soul, but He truly does so to a weak soul, for God is Mercy, and never does the misery of a soul separate from God.[80]

In a letter written to a nun during Paschaltide, he gives a just commentary on the Augustinian adage:

Alleluia! I send you this joyful good wish from the bottom of my heart. The alleluia announces to the saints and to us the triumph of Him "Who loved us and delivered Himself for us."[81]

I pray that this first Lent may be fruitful for you and fill your heart with a sincere love for Jesus. Saint Augustine writes, "Love and do what you will." That is true, for a sincere love of God makes us leave ourselves and give ourselves to Jesus. The interests of Jesus become ours, and as soon as we know that anything gives Him pleasure, real love does not hesitate an instant to think whether the thing demanded pleases us or not; the one thought is: "will that give pleasure to the One Who is the Object of my love?" You will learn by experience that this sincere love of

Jesus, in its simplicity, will settle all your difficulties, for our difficulties come from our self-love, and the sincere love of Jesus destroys self-love. I say that you will have no difficulties, but I do not say that you will have neither crosses nor trials; but when one has real love, "the difficulty is loved."[82] Trials cease to be difficulties, for nothing is difficult for love.[83]

Thus, then, love is only proved by generous fidelity to the Divine good pleasure. He writes to a very young girl:

Try to prove your love of Jesus by your fidelity. REAL love consists in doing the will of the one we love, and the will of Jesus is that you imitate Him, Who at each moment could say, "I do always the things that please My Father."[84]

And again to the same:

Try to show your gratitude to Jesus Christ by great fidelity in all things. My dear child, we must never forget that true piety does not consist only in saying long prayers, but *above all* in showing our love to Jesus by the care and fidelity we take to do His holy will. For you, His will is manifested in your keeping house and your duties of state. Then, the more you love Jesus, the more faithful you will be to give yourself up entirely to carrying out His will.[85]

He writes to a student:

What you tell me of your progress in your studies much consoles me, for true piety, the *real* love of Jesus urges us ever to do our best to fulfill our duties of state.[86]

He makes this fidelity the object of his prayer for the souls confided to him:

The collect for the Second Mass on Christmas Day asks that we may show forth in our actions what shines in our minds by faith; that is my New Year's wish for you all.[87]

He wants this fidelity to be total, absolute, even in small things, for the Divine Will is contained in them. He writes to a nun:

You ought not to be discouraged, nor think that you are going back; but you are not making the progress that I should like to see you make. I would have you belong to the Good God entirely for you are able to love Him dearly. You ought to dread the least little voluntary infidelity towards Our Lord, and accustom yourself to be faithful, out of love, even in the smallest things. Make your particular examen on this.[88]

And to another:

Be *faithful in little things*, not out of meticulousness, but out of love. Do this to prove to Our Lord that you have the love of a spouse for Him.[89]

In certain points of detail, he insists on this fidelity because he sees in it a more decisive and desirable orientation for the soul:

Regularity and fidelity in rising in the morning are of capital importance.

And in a happy phrase, he shows the reason:

It is a question of giving the first moments of the day to Our Lord or to His enemy, and the whole day bears the reflection of this first choice.[90]

He writes to a married woman:

God loves you, for you are straightforward, and do your duty for love of Him. I recommend you to direct your day each morning by an act of love towards God, and then, during the day, to think of Him from time to time. He gazes unceasingly upon you, and He so much loves to have us think of Him. "Think of Me," He told a Saint, "and I will think of thee."[91]

Constant and likewise generous fidelity:

* I do hope you are very faithful to Our Lord even in the midst of the darkness through which He so often wishes to lead you. "For though I should walk in the midst of the shadow of death, I will fear no evils for Thou art with me..."[92] I pray daily for you, and do hope you are keeping up your courage despite the dryness of your ordinary life.[93]

That he was inspired by a holy horror of tepidity, that rust of the heart which gradually destroys love, need not surprise us. "Piety without the spirit of sacrifice," he often said, "is like an organism without a backbone." In the following letter he puts the soul on her guard against the oft-recurring danger of mediocrity, and his zeal for God's glory gives a somewhat vehement tone to his warning. He writes to a Benedictine nun:

Your kind letter gave me great pleasure. I can say with Saint John, "I have no greater grace than this, to hear that my children walk in truth."[94]

Our vocation is so beautiful that my greatest sorrow is to see anyone lose a particle of the grace and joy contained in our Rule and our life, for want of corresponding to God's goodness. We are so weak, yes, so weak! If Our Lord should withdraw His hand for a second, we should be capable of every sin, so that no weakness astonishes me, and it does not prevent Our Lord from loving us all the same and from giving Himself to us. But I do not understand a monk or nun making a voluntary reserve. I cannot conceive how a person who has received Our Lord in Holy Communion, and to whom He has given all, even His Precious Blood, can say afterwards, "I know that would give pleasure to Our Lord, but I will not do it." A person living in this disposition will never be anything but a tepid monk or nun. Of such, God said, "I would thou wert cold or hot, but because thou art lukewarm... I will begin to vomit thee out of my mouth."[95] I love sinners dearly, I am never so happy as when I can help them and can feel like the Good Shepherd Who left the ninety-nine sheep in the desert to go after the lost sheep, but I confess to you that I have to make a supreme effort to be even polite to indifferent religious who serve the Lord above all for their own satisfaction, and do not wish to follow Him in His humiliation and His generosity.[96]

3. *Fidelity and Liberty of Spirit*

That generous fidelity which Dom Marmion demands for so many reasons, he wishes to be an enlightened fidelity. Rarely has such keen solicitude been exerted in warning the soul against the erroneous conception that places *all* perfection in *merely outward and material fidelity* to the Divine will.

"Although the word I use is severe," he said when speaking on this matter, "I do not hesitate to pronounce it: the abovesaid prejudicial idea would border upon pharisaism, or would risk leading to it, and that would be a great danger."[97]

Your retreat resolution, "To do in all things what is most pleasing to Our Lord," is excellent. I would not like to see a pharisaical fidelity in you, but I very much want you to be faithful out of love.[98]

He wrote again:

What is important in our observance is the *inner principle* that animates us. The Pharisees observed all things exactly but it was that they might be seen and applauded by the multitude, and this moral deviation utterly spoiled all their works... Outward observance, sought after for its own sake, without the inward love which quickens it, is a formal show—even a Pharisaical show... The ideal we ought to have in view is the exactitude of love... The interior life must be the soul of our exterior fidelity. It must be the result, the fruit and manifestation of the faith, confidence, and love that govern our heart... Fidelity is the most precious and delicate flower of love here below...

In this exactitude which is born of love there is something easy, wide, free, lovable, joyous.[99]

He has said too much on this theme in more than one place in his works for us to need to insist upon it. He is intent on doing away with scruples:

An excessive meticulousness only creates difficulties where there are none.[100]

Saint Francis de Sales, the holy Bishop of Geneva, wrote to Madame de la Fléchère: "I should like to have a good hammer to blunt the edge of your mind which is too subtle in the thought of your advancement. I have told you so often that we must set about our devotions in simple good faith and, as they say, in a 'wholesale' manner. If you do well, praise God for it; if you do badly, humble yourself. I am well aware that you would not do ill wilfully. Have no fear then, and do not be so ready to tease your dear conscience, for you know too well that after all your efforts, there is nothing more for you to do than to implore the love of Him Who only desires you to give Him yours."[101]

Dom Marmion speaks in the same strain. To a nun of good will whom he saw was forever embarrassing herself in a complicated searching out of the motives of her actions, he takes a firm and reassuring tone. She must free her soul from the trammels which impede its flight. The letter is dated December 21, 1922, a month before his death:

The great grace of the Nativity is one which will deliver you from all your troubles. "That new birth will deliver you from the yoke of the old bondage."[102] It is the grace of being born with Jesus, to that liberty of the *children* of God. "Unless you become as little children, you shall not enter into the Kingdom of Heaven." It is this spiritual *childhood* that is wanting to you. A child receives simply and unquestioningly what his father says to him; you, on the contrary, make yourself a doctor of the law. You examine minutely all that is said to you, you lose yourself in details. God is too *pure*, too noble to concern Himself with all these trifles, these distinctions. Take the advice that is offered you in the *wide* and natural sense in which it is given, and leave the rest to God. The more of a child you are, the more light and joy you will have; the more you play the advocate, the jurist, the more you will entangle yourself in a mesh of details. Do not seek too much for the *motives* of your actions; Look at God, and He will be Himself your motive. In a word, be a good child and Jesus will be pleased to rest in your heart. He does not like bluestockings.[103]

The life of union with God cannot but blossom out in peace and joy:

* I am so glad to hear that your soul is in peace. "Seek after peace and pursue it."[104] God would have us do all in our power to be in peace, in order to communicate Himself to our souls. "The Lord is not in the earthquake."

You must not go back on the past, God does not wish it, except in a general way, just to humble yourself *before Him*, casting yourself at His feet as a poor sinner and asking His pardon. "O God, be merciful to me a sinner."[105]

He writes to a nun:

A little word, to tell you what joy your letter caused me. I long so much to see you given up to Our Lord in holy and ever increasing joy. The more you are united to Jesus, the more you will be a child of God—for He is by essence *Filius Dei*, Son of God—and the note of the child of the Heavenly Father is "the holy liberty of the children of God." I say to you then, with my dear Saint Paul, "Be ye therefore followers of God, and walk in love as most dear children." Despise the vain fears that the enemy puts into your soul and at these moments, with Saint Augustine, cast yourself into the arms of the Heavenly Father.[106]

Many of his letters are full of these counsels which reassure and set free, counsels of a quite "Columbanian" flavor as certain of those under his direction used to say. To a young girl:

Be very faithful, but without scruples, to your spiritual exercises. Remain in peace; during the day often make acts of submission and abandon to God's holy will, and fear nothing.[107]

He gives he same counsel to a contemplative nun:

You need a great fidelity, but without constraint or scruple, for the more one is a child of the Heavenly Father, the more one enjoys the holy liberty of His children.[108]

This liberty of heart ought to extend even to good works voluntarily chosen, nay even to practices which one finds impossible to perform; it is above all things important to keep in peace and in the spirit of abandonment to Providence:

It is good to make little mortifications from time to time out of love, but they must be made with entire liberty of heart, without thinking that if we omit one or another that presents itself, we are doing wrong. The devil sometimes thus tries to falsify our conscience and to make us believe we are doing wrong if we omit a mortification that comes our way. It is good to make them sometimes, and at other times it is good to omit them in order to keep our liberty of heart.[109]

He writes excellently to a Carmelite Prioress:

If experience shows you that you cannot fast, you must bow before the will of God Who wishes more for the sacrifice of your attraction and your will than for the sacrifices which are born of austerity.[110]

Those of a right way of thinking will not put a wrong construction on what Dom Marmion says. Liberty of spirit, far from being relaxation, infidelity or want of zeal is, on the contrary, but the result of habitual fidelity to love; it is "an adhesion to the Divine Will beyond human means of sanctification."[111] Far from lessening fidelity, it gives its true meaning and safeguards "the primacy of the inner life."

4. *In Christ Jesus*

A lofty ideal is this union with God, this full conformity of will, in the love that yields up everything, an altogether supernatural ideal but one which God Himself has rendered accessible through His Son Jesus. More than once in the pages just cited we have seen how Dom Marmion makes the eyes of the soul rest upon Christ, the Incarnate Word, Source of all grace, the infallible Way which leads to the Father and brings the soul into the Bosom of God. He possessed a happy understanding of this doctrine; being the dominant thought of his whole life and the inspiration of all his spiritual works it could not fail to be met with in his letters. The life of Christ by which he lived intensely inspired more than one beautiful page where assuredly it is the result of his own personal experiences which he gives us, often unawares to himself.

In a few full and concise pages which form a whole rule of life Dom Marmion has gathered together the main points of his doctrine on this subject:

I cannot tell you how happy I am in seeing the graces which the Father is giving you through His Son, for in spite of your misery He is leading you in His Spirit by the best of all ways, by

Jesus, to the Father, in joyful and humble dependence on Him...
Let us remain closely united "in the bosom of the Father"[112]
through Jesus Christ.[113]

**To a Carmelite monk who asks him "to sum up in a few lines his
teaching on Christ and the spiritual life," he traces out this full and
vigorous synthesis:**

I am rejoiced to see that the Holy Spirit is making you understand that we have *all* in Jesus Christ. For this knowledge is the
grain of mustard seed Our Lord speaks of, which to begin with
is very small, then, on being cultivated, becomes a great tree.

Here, in two words, is what I try to teach:

Jesus Christ is Infinite Holiness, *Tu solus Sanctus, Jesu Christe.*

But He is not only holy in Himself; He has been given to us
to be *our* holiness, "Christ Jesus, Who of God is made unto us
wisdom, and justice, and SANCTIFICATION and redemption."[114]

He is our holiness:

1. As perfect *model*: "Predestined to be made conformable to
the image of His Son."[115] God finds in Him all His delights:
"This is My beloved Son, in Whom I am well pleased."[116] He
finds them in us according to the degree of our likeness to Jesus.

2. *As means of union with God.* In Jesus the divine nature and
the human nature are united in oneness of Person, and we are
united with the Divinity in the measure of our union with the
Sacred Humanity of Jesus: "Cornerstone that makest both one."[117]
It is by sanctifying grace that this union with God is brought
about, and this grace is the work of the Blessed Trinity in us.

3. However the effusion of this grace depends on Jesus Christ:
a) it is He who has merited it; *b*) it is He who applies it through
His Sacred Humanity; *c*) this grace tends to reproduce in us the
features of Jesus Christ; *d*) the more we lean upon Him, the
more abundant is this grace. In fact this grace, poured forth
without measure in the Sacred Humanity, is communicated to

His members in the measure of their union with Him by faith and love: "I am the Vine: you the branches."[118]

All the graces that we receive tend to make of us by grace [of adoption] what Jesus is by nature—children of God.

That is why this *same* Holy Spirit Who was, in Jesus, the principle of His whole human life, is given to us: "Because you are sons, God hath sent the Spirit of His Son into your hearts, crying: Abba, Father."[119] It is this Holy Spirit Who achieves in us the image of Jesus and fills us with His life: "the Spirit gives life."[120]

There in a few words is all that I know.[121]

What he also knows, and no less excellently how to explain, is the soul's attitude in face of the ineffable mystery of the Incarnate Word:

I have been praying a great deal for you, for Our Lord always gives me the longing for your perfection. It seems to me that, for you, the cult of Jesus in His Divinity and in His Humanity is the synthesis of perfection. In His *Divinity*: adoration, utter humility, boundless confidence in His power, His goodness, His faithfulness. In His *Humanity*: to find in Him all that our human hearts can ask of love, affection, and sympathy, for He is as truly man—Son of man—as He is God. And as His human nature is really distinct from His Divine nature and remains, without being confounded, in the unity of His Divine Person, so His human love is truly distinct from His Divine love, although in perfect accord with it, being the expression, under a human form, of His Divine love. The humanity of Jesus is the door whereby we enter into the sanctuary of His Divinity: "I am the Door";[122] it is the translation, in human and intelligible words, of that Infinite and incomprehensible Word: "The only begotten Son Who is in the bosom of the Father."[123]

Love unifies all this in one single act. Here then is all there is to
say: "Love Jesus Christ."

You will ask me, my child, like the disciples to Saint John:
"Why do you always repeat the same thing to me." It is because
this is all I know, and this contains everything: "I judged not
myself to know anything among you, but Jesus Christ, and Him
crucified."[124] It is because, while loving you more than ever, I
no longer feel the need to write to you much. I feel that I have
cooperated a little, with Our Lord, to make enter into your heart
and be engraved upon it this great principle that *Jesus is all*, and
I see that my part now is to make this divine seed germinate by
my prayers, and I do so more than ever and, it seems to me,
with more fervor and love.

May God bless you, my child, and may He make of you the
saint that I dream in my prayers.[125]

**Thus the whole of the interior life leads up to the life of union
with Christ:**

I thank Our Lord with all my heart that He unites you so
closely to His Sacred Heart and makes you understand more
and more the need you have to live very near to Him. Indeed,
my daughter, the inner life becomes very simple from the
moment we understand that it consists entirely in losing oneself
in Jesus Christ, making only one heart, one soul, one will with
His own. This is not done once and for all, "one buries oneself
more and more in this holy will" as Saint Chantal so truly said,
but one can do nothing apart from it.[126]

**To lose oneself in Jesus Christ; to be incorporated in Him,
identified with Him, to abide in union with Him: such is the
teaching that Dom Marmion, after the example of Saint John and
Saint Paul, did not cease to give. He was content with showing
Christ as the model of the virtues we must imitate; he especially**

laid emphasis—and here we have one of the characteristics of his teaching—on *the sanctifying power of the Sacred Humanity*. He has shown, with particular delectation springing from the vivacity of his faith,[127] how Christ operates the work of sanctification deep down in the soul wholly yielded up to the action of His Spirit:

There is, concerning your spiritual life, one truth which I want to impress upon your soul. All our efforts are only of any avail in as far as Jesus Christ acts in us and helps us: "I am the Vine; you the branches. As the branches cannot bear any fruit unless they abide in the vine, neither can you do anything good unless you abide in Me. For without Me you can do nothing."[128] Indeed Saint Paul tells us that "God has given us His Son Jesus to be *our* Wisdom, *our* Justice, *our* Sanctification, *our* Redemption."[129] You have still too much confidence in your own activity, and consequently, you do not lean enough upon Him, you do not put yourself enough in His hands.[130]

This last remark is one to be borne in mind: in order for Christ's action in the soul to be fruitful, all the obstacles opposed to the freedom of its operation must be removed:

* The Sacred Humanity had no human personality[131] (it is that *human personality* that is the object of our self-love and all its consequences, sensitiveness, susceptibility, etc.; we must immolate it to the Divine Spouse, the Word, and thus all such barriers are broken down). And so this Sacred Humanity gave itself to the Divine Spouse, the Word, without *any barrier*. This is your example. If you could dash every child born of self-love against the Rock,[132] Christ, your union would be perfect.[133]

He writes to another:

If you abandon yourself without reserve to the Divine action of the Sacred Humanity of Jesus, He will carry you along with Him in that Divine current which ever flows like an impetuous torrent in the bosom of the Word. There your little personality will be lost and will disappear in deep adoration and perfect love; thus all that comes from this personality (self-love, susceptibility, sadness, etc.) will be destroyed.[134]

A deep thought which Dom Marmion develops after his own manner in a letter to a nun:

One must not, before beginning any action, give in to nature, but first unite one's self to Our Lord. Before taking up an occupation, kneel down at Christ's feet and say to Him: "My Jesus, I leave there my natural activity, I want to do this thing solely for You, and I unite myself to You." And if during the occupation, you feel that you are letting yourself be carried away by nature, go back to Our Lord. It must not be A— [name of the religious] who is acting, for that would be good for nothing; but it must be Jesus who acts through A—, then it will be excellent.

There are some people who have a great deal of activity; they pray, mortify themselves, and give themselves up to good works; they advance but rather limpingly, because their activity is partly human. There are others whom God has taken in hand, and they advance very quickly, because He Himself acts in them. But before reaching this second state, there is much to suffer, for God must first make the soul feel that she is nothing and can do nothing; she must needs be able to say in all sincerity, "I am brought to nothing, and I knew not. I am become as a beast before Thee."[135]

My dear child, it is this that the Good God is about to do in you, and you will have much to suffer before arriving at this result; but do not be alarmed if you feel everything is boiling over in you; don't be discouraged if next you feel your incapacity, for God after having as it were annihilated your human activity, your natural energies, will Himself take your soul and bring it to union with Him. When you make the Way of the Cross, unite yourself to the sentiments that our dear Savior had; it cannot fail to please the Eternal Father, if we offer to Him the image of His Son. At the 14th station, we see Our Lord's body *exinanitum*, but after three days, He comes forth from the tomb, full of life, of splendid life. It will be the same for us too; if we let God act in us, after He has destroyed all there is that is human and natural in us, we shall be filled with His life; it will then be the realization of these words, *Christ is my life.*[136]

This is what you must arrive at; the Eternal Father wishes to see in you only His Son. Remember Saint Paul's words: "That I may be found in Him."[137] That is your way, my child. Your personality is still too strong; keep before the eyes of your soul the ideal that is to be found in Jesus Christ, where all comes from the Word without there being a human personality in Christ.[138] I recommend you to take each of your faculties every morning and lay them down at Christ's feet, that all may come from Him and that you no longer act except out of love for Him.[139]

He writes in another letter:

The great thing for you is to understand the riches you have in Our Lord. He is your Spouse, consequently all His riches are yours. But they must be turned to account. And for that you need two things—confident abandon and identity with Our Lord. This union depends much more on Him than on you, He has said, "My Father hath not left me alone: for I do always the things that please Him."[140] Meditate a little on these words, my dear child. Look at God in all that you do, and do all for love—prayer, work, school, recreation, etc. Then Our Lord will come to you, "If any one love Me, My Father will love him, and we will come to him, and make our abode with him."[141]

This union with Our Lord is not incompatible with our occupations. The more I see of souls, the more I am assured that exterior circumstances cannot hurt this union.[142]

Let the soul therefore give herself up without fear to the sovereignly efficacious operation of the Sacred Humanity; is not Christ Infallible Wisdom and Eternal Love? To a nun:

Let *Jesus* be the absolute Master of your inner life, and He will teach you all the secrets of His love. He has said, "Neither doth anyone know *the Father*, but the Son, and he to whom it shall please the Son to reveal Him."[143] Think well on that, for our Heavenly Father is the supreme End of the spiritual life.[144]

Seek Christ in everything. "He must increase, we must disappear."[145] Let us live for the Father in Jesus, with Him, for Him; let all the operations of our hearts ever mount towards Him.[146]

At the Feast of the Nativity these are his wishes for a Happy Christmas:

* The little Infant Who is in our heart is gazing on the Face of His Father, "In the presence of God for us."[147] He *sees* in His Father's Eternal love the place you occupy, God's plan for you, a plan so minute that "not a hair of your head falls without Him." Give yourself up to Jesus, the Eternal Wisdom in order that He may lead you and guide you to the fulfillment of that ideal.[148]

It is above all in Eucharistic Communion that Christ's action in the soul is particularly efficacious and fruitful:

If you yield yourself up every morning without reserve to Jesus, at Holy Communion, He will be your Master in the spiritual life. He alone knows what each one needs, and if you place yourself at His *entire disposal*, He will do the rest... The spiritual life is simple, like God Himself, once that Jesus is the whole life of our soul. Every day lay down your life in the sepulchre with Jesus, at the 14th Station of the Cross, by renewing your baptismal promises; then take the risen life of Jesus as the focus of your life, and all will go well.[149]

He writes to one of his monks:

I rejoice greatly to see that everything goes on so well. This need of God shows that His Spirit is in the depth of your heart. In the midst of this *multiplicity* of duties, seek *unity* by *great* purity of intention. We are "members of Jesus Christ," and consequently we have a right to all that He does in our name. It is so sweet to close the eyes of the soul, to kiss His Feet, and let Him pray and love in our name.[150]

Upon this theme, Dom Marmion is tireless; we regret to have to make a limited choice out of so many riches:

Every day, in Holy Communion, Christ gives Himself entirely to us; He takes us and gives us to the Word. If our whole day could flow from our Communion of the morning, little by little, Christ would transform us and raise us to sublime holiness. What we cannot do, Jesus does for us. In the world, the bridegroom is the strength of his bride who is weak, and the more powerless she is, the more he acts for her. You are, by your religious profession, the bride of Christ. The more weak, miserable, powerless you are, the more Christ becomes your strength, the more He supplies for you... When you cannot say the prayers that you would wish, Jesus says them for you.

As for me, if you asked me in what the spiritual life consists, I should say, "It is very simple, it is summarized in one word: Christ." In his Epistle to the Galatians, Saint Paul, after having said all that Christ is for us, sums up his thought in this beautiful text, "And whosoever shall follow this rule, peace on them and mercy."[151] Yes, those who seek Christ have peace and mercy.[152]

   * God has poured forth all "the treasures of His Wisdom and of His Science"[153] on the Sacred Humanity of Jesus Christ because of its union with the Word, and *the measure of His gifts to*

us, is the degree of our union with this same Word. Now this union with the Word is effected by the power and *efficacy of the Sacred Humanity, especially in Holy Communion.* What we have to do is to maintain ourselves, through the Sacred Humanity in an habitual state of absolute adoration and SUBMISSION to the Word, Who resides within us. Our life must be an *Amen* ever echoing the wishes and designs of that Word on us. A soul once arrived at that state, becomes the object of God's best gifts.[154]

And on another occasion he wrote:

Lend your voice to the Word that He may use it as His organ to praise His Father.[155]

For love's sake, the Humanity in Jesus was fully yielded up to the action of the Word; at this divine furnace the soul ought to enkindle her love, the principle of her union with God:

I want you, my child, to apply yourself with order and attention to act *solely* out of love for God in all that you do. Each action done out of pure love is an act of pure love of God, and the more this act costs you, the greater and more meritorious is the love. Thus it was upon the cross that Our Lord showed most love. What costs nothing is worth nothing.[156]

But where are we to find this pure love? We have it neither of ourselves, nor in ourselves. We shall find it in the Sacred Heart of Jesus Which is an infinite furnace of love, and as you receive this Sacred Heart so often in Holy Communion, you have only to place your heart in the center of this Divine Heart in order to love with Its love. Oh yes, my child, the Sacred Heart is an *infinite* treasury of Divine love, and this Heart *is ours, It abides always in us.* "He that eateth My flesh, and drinketh My blood, abideth in Me, and I in him." Unite yourself then very often with the Sacred Heart, and love with It and by It.

This is *a great secret.* Here are the words of Saint Ambrose: "The mouth of Jesus on the cross has become our mouth, and with it we speak to the Father to appease His wrath; His Heart pierced by the lance has become our heart and with it we love the Father." Yes, Jesus came upon this earth for that alone. "I am come to cast fire (the fire of love) on the earth; and what will I, but that it be kindled?"[157]

Dom Marmion stirs up this fire by a "program of love" and union which he traces out for a soul eager for perfection. This program is a commentary, concise but profound, of the great precept, "Thou shall love the Lord thy God with all thy heart..." He begins by showing the perfect fulfillment of this precept in Jesus become "the one and only model" and "center of love."

On rising, in union with the Sacred Heart of Jesus, Whose first movement was an impulse of love by which He offered Himself without reserve to His Father, say, "Behold, I come to do Thy will, O God."

On beginning the day, on entering the oratory, *unite* your heart closely with the Heart of Jesus. This Heart was a glowing center of love, for Jesus loved His Father *with all His Heart.*

This love of your heart ought to shine out in the love *of your whole soul,* by employing your soul and all its faculties in prayer and the Divine Praise. Jesus loved His Father with all His Soul.

During the day, this love of your heart ought also to shine out in the work of obedience done *with all your strength.* Jesus worked for love of His Father with all His strength.

Finally, *throughout* the day, let your love urge you to occupy your mind with the thought of God, with studying His perfections, and with all that relates to His service. That is loving God *with all one's mind.* The Spirit of Jesus was ever plunged in the contemplation of His Father.

During the day, be faithful to "direct" your different actions according to the prescriptions of your holy Rule.

Often go back, by a spiritual Communion, to that center of love which is the Sacred Heart of Jesus. All *our* life ought to be passed in this sweet intercourse with *the Spouse of our souls, Jesus.*[158]

All this magnificent doctrine is summed up in this thought:

Do all your actions as far as possible out of *pure love of God, and in union with the perfect dispositions of the Sacred Heart of Jesus.*[159]

A sentence which he expressed more profoundly in these terms:

As for us, let us ever keep our gaze fixed upon the face (i.e., the good pleasure) of the Father through the eyes of Jesus Christ: "Seek His face evermore."[160]

5. *"Programs" and "Directives"*

More than once, those eager for perfection begged Dom Marmion for "programs" of union with God. We have already come across several of these syntheses where Dom Marmion gathers up in clear concise forms, and with the art that was all his own, the essentials of a doctrine, adapting it to the particular needs of his correspondents.

Here we have others, given in chronological order, which many will be glad to read; in spite of what may be especially applicable to the persons to whom he wrote, we shall here find again the fundamental thoughts set forth in the preceding chapters. These pages form the natural supplement of this section.

At the time of his departure for Louvain, in April 1899, he is begged by one of his confreres to leave him "a few general principles of religious life." He condenses them in these lines:

1. The substance of every seriously devout life is the faithful accomplishment of God's *known will.* This will is manifested in *a)* the commandments; *b)* the evangelical counsels; *c)* for us, in

our Rule and the orders of Superiors. All the rest is accidental, and of more or less importance according as it helps us to do what is substantial.

2. Fidelity to religious duties, Divine Office, mental prayer, spiritual reading, is the source of the strength we need to carry out this will of God.

That is why, although these practices are not the substance of sanctity, negligence in these duties leads inevitably to the more or less grave violation of the intrinsic obligations, and to the ruin of spiritual life.

3. True love of God in the heart of one who has gravely sinned ought to take the form of compunction. Not that compunction ought to be the exclusive form, but the basis, the point to which he ever returns: "DAILY to confess one's past sins with tears and sighs to God."[161]

4. When one has sinned much, he ought not to be surprised to find himself deprived of savor and sweetness in his devotions. This lost grace must be expiated or redeemed by long fidelity.

5. Among practices of piety, the most fruitful is the union of our life and sentiments with those of Jesus Christ. "Let this mind be in you which was also in Christ Jesus."[162] "No man cometh *to the Father, but by Me*."[163] "I am the Way."[164] "By Him, and with Him, and in Him, is to Thee, God the Father Almighty... ALL honor and glory."[165]

In 1915, one of his spiritual daughters brought Dom Marmion a small picture and asked him to write on the back of it a "resume of the spiritual life." With a stroke of the pen he traced these lines:

1. Seek God alone and His good pleasure.
2. Seek God by the Way—Jesus Christ.
3. Look at God much more than at yourself. See all things,

even your faults and miseries, in Him. His mercy is an ocean which will drown them all.

4. Pray much for him who will never forget you before God.

April 6, 1916.—To a person in the world:

You ask me, my dear daughter, to give you some advice for the direction of your life. This is what I write to you in God's presence:

1. God has been *very good* to you, for He has given you light and grace to understand that *true piety* consists much less in a great number of prayers and practices than in the sincere and honest seeking after His Holy will. This "orientation," this direction of our life and activity to His good pleasure is the *essence* of the spiritual life. Prayers, Sacraments, practices are the *means* to strengthen and sustain us in this seeking.

2. God, however, wills that each one, according to his or her vocation and circumstances, should offer Him daily the homage of adoration and prayer, and He exacts great fidelity in this matter. Not many prayers, but much fidelity in saying them. When I see you, we will have a talk together about what is most suitable for you to undertake. Nothing is a greater help to us than to assist at Holy Mass.

3. One practice I recommend to you above all is that of ejaculatory prayers.

4. A little spiritual reading would help you very much in your good resolutions.

5. Your failings come from one common source—a want of *interior mortification* prevents you from controlling the movements of your heart, of your tongue and of your activity. Creature of impulse as you are, you have not learnt to make the sacrifice of your first movements. Try little by little to make Jesus so much *the Master*, the Lord of your inner life, that He may keep you, guide you, and unite you to Himself in His perfect submission to His Father.

You love Our Lord dearly and *He loves you*, but you must be more in His hands. Once you are in Our Lord's hands and submissive to His inspirations, you will have that equilibrium, that evenness of mind which are so important for those who have to govern others and do good to them.

When I see you, I will explain to you further what I have just written.

May 25, 1919.—To the mother of a family:

Your kind letter gave me so much pleasure because I see you are seeking God with sincerity. I tell you in all simplicity that I believe God loves you dearly and that the little worries of this life form that portion of the cross of Jesus which is to unite you to Him.

God does not ask a married woman of the world for the austerities and mortifications that may be practised by those living in the cloister. But He sends them other trials adapted to their state and which render them so agreeable to His Divine Majesty. Our Lord asks of you:

1. To accept daily the sufferings, the duties and the joys that He sends you, as Jesus accepted all that came to Him from His Father. When Saint Peter wanted to turn Him away from His Passion, on account of his great affection for Him, Jesus answered him, "The chalice *which My Father hath given Me*, shall I not drink it?" There, my daughter, is the answer you ought to give when you seem to be overwhelmed with suffering.

2. The perfect fulfillment of your duties:

a) Towards God.—Prayer, Mass, Holy Communion, not too many prayers, but great fidelity in saying those which it is a duty to offer to God, above all family prayers.

b) Towards your neighbor.—Towards your husband. Marriage, says Saint Paul, is the image of Christ's union with the Church, and the Sacrament of marriage gives you a *continual participation* in the union of Jesus and His Church. Jesus so loved His Church that He died for her, and she, in return, loves Him as her God and her Bridegroom. Thus you should love your husband as representing Christ for you.

Towards your children. The grace of motherhood has its origin in the Heart of God and He puts it in the mother's heart in order that she may love and guide her children according to the Divine good pleasure.

c) *Towards yourself.*—At present no other mortifications are necessary for you than those which God sends you daily. But you must sanctify them by uniting them to the sufferings of Jesus Christ.

Be joyful and gay, natural and straightforward as you are, and God will bless you.

June 7, 1922.—To a person in the world:

For you, this is your way:

1. United to Jesus and leaning upon His love and upon His merits, go to the Father with a childlike love. This intention of pleasing God in all things uplifts and simplifies our whole life.

2. Great submission to God in all that happens to you; accept likewise the joys that our Heavenly Father sends you, with a simple gaiety, without being *too wrapped up in pleasures*, says Saint Benedict.[166]

3. Make from time to time, in the course of the day, a spiritual Communion as the starting point of a fresh impetus towards God.

4. If you fall into some fault or failing, do not be astonished, but ask Our Father's forgiveness with great simplicity, and then, go forward. Be yourself, for N— is very good and God loves N— united to Jesus.

5. Accept as penance what is troublesome in your responsibilities.

CHAPTER III

CONDITIONS FOR PROGRESS IN THE LIFE OF UNION WITH GOD

1. *The Desire for Perfection*

A generously faithful and loving adhesion to the Divine will in conformity with the mind of Christ: such is the essence of the life of union with God.

Like all life, the life of union with God is subject to a law of growth whose conditions are duly determined and to which the soul must voluntarily submit. As gathered from Dom Marmion's letters, these conditions may be reduced to two, in the following logical order: the desire for perfection, and then detachment and renunciation, above all by the practice of patience.[167]

The desire for perfection is the initial point; detachment does away with the obstacles that oppose the soul's progress.

In order to arouse the longing for perfection, to stimulate the dawning ardor of holy ambitions, Dom Marmion could find no better plan than to unveil the supernatural greatness of a life of union with God; and the passion which possesses him for souls gives a somewhat vehement tone to his appeal.

He writes to a religious:

The Benedictine virgin is not called to seek the Spouse in the streets and public places of the town, like the Sister of Charity,

46

but in the nuptial chamber of prayer and recollection. It is not in the company of men, even the holiest, that her life is spent but "her conversation must be with the angels."[168] Oh, my child, you have been called to the best part, "The lines are fallen unto me in goodly places."[169] Our Lord receives more glory from a soul that serves Him perfectly than from a thousand others that lead a mediocre spiritual life.

In order to give more weight to this deep teaching, his humility supports it upon the authority of two masters whose doctrine is universally recognized:

The Venerable Louis de Blois tells us that those who are united to God without intermediary and leave Him free to act in them, are very dear to the Lord and do more for the Church in one hour than others, less favored, in many years.[170] "When the soul has reached perfect union," writes Saint John of the Cross, "the least movement of pure love is worth more in God's sight and is more profitable to the whole Church than all the other virtues put together."[171]

And here is the urgent conclusion to his letter:

I have a great longing to see you become a perfect religious, for the contemplative virgin cannot, like the Sister of Charity, acquire merit by serving Our Lord in the person of the poor and suffering; that is why if she does not glorify God by a life of great perfection, she will have done little for Him during her life, but if she gives herself generously to Jesus Christ, allowing Him to do what He wills in her, and to immolate her according to the designs of His Eternal Wisdom, oh! then the eye of faith can alone judge of the value and usefulness of such a life in God's sight.[172]

Put more concisely, the same thought is found again in a note written to a nun about to pronounce her Vows of religion:

For you, my prayer will be, "Make of us, O Lord, an oblation worthy to be offered to Thee for evermore."[173] When one understands the greatness and sublimity of our vocation, this *entire* and unconditional oblation to the glory of Jesus in leaving Him *carte blanche* to dispose of all that He finds in us; when one lives always at the height of this oblation in humility and obedience, one does *great things* for His glory. He is the "Beginning"—"I am the beginning, Who also speak unto you"[174]—and all that does not come from Him is doomed to failure.[175]

I pray for you that you may become a real saint. A real saint gives more glory to God and saves more souls than a thousand ordinary souls.[176]

I have just been celebrating Mass for *us*. I hope Our Lord will have given you what I should have liked to give you, namely an increase of knowledge and love of the Blessed Trinity. May Our Lord bless you, and give you grace to respond perfectly to His expectations.[177]

At the time of my last visit, I saw with joy that you have given yourself without reserve to Jesus and, if you are faithful, you will attain to a great union with Him. You are on the right road.[178]

The expression "to give oneself without reserve"—Dom Marmion often underlines these two last words—is found again and again under his pen, as also the expression, "to yield oneself up totally to Jesus Christ." These terms have with him a very exact meaning; they denote the initial and resolute movement of the soul eager to come to the perfection of the life of union. Dom Marmion insists a great deal on this disposition; he makes it an indispensable condition of spiritual progress. Hence in his letters, these good wishes so often renewed:

* January 1, 1907.—May God bless you and take you *all to* Himself.

* March 14, 1914.—May God bless and guard you and lead you to His perfect love.

An apparently strange thing, he met with some persons who imagined there was a taint of egoism in aiming at high perfection. Dom Marmion resolutely confutes this error. The seeking after holiness has its mainspring in the very will of God:

* There is nothing selfish in seeking high perfection, as it gives such glory to God. "In this is My Father glorified that you bear *much* fruit," so "Be ye *perfect*, as also your heavenly Father is perfect." Jesus did not die merely to save us, but above all to sanctify His Church. Our sanctification is the triumph of His precious Blood—a glory for *all* eternity.[179]

The Divine will on one hand, the infinite power of the grace of Jesus on the other. Dom Marmion constantly appeals to these two motives to intensify and maintain in souls an ardent longing for union with God. After having proclaimed, in the words of Saint Paul, the greatness of Christ's victories, he exclaims: "Why then is it that pusillanimous souls are to be found who say that holiness is not for them, that perfection is something beyond their power, who say, when one speaks to them of perfection: 'It is not for me; I could never arrive at sanctity.' Do you know what makes them speak thus? It is their lack of faith in the efficacy of Christ's merits. For it is the will of God that all should be holy: 'For this is the will of God, your sanctification.'[180] It is Our Lord's precept: 'Be ye therefore perfect, as also your Heavenly Father is perfect.' But we too often forget the Divine Plan; we forget that holiness for us is a supernatural holiness of which the source is only in Jesus Christ, our Chief and our Head; we do a wrong to Christ's infinite merits and inexhaustible satisfaction. Doubtless, by ourselves, we can do nothing in the way of grace or perfection; Our Lord expressly tells us so. *Without Me you can do* NOTHING.[181] And Saint Augustine, commenting on this text, adds: 'Whether things be small or great, nothing can be done without Him Who has made all things.'[182] That is so true! Whether it concerns great things or small, we can do nothing without Christ. But by dying for us, Christ has given us free and confident access to the Father, and through Him there is no grace for which we cannot hope. Souls of little faith, why do we doubt of God, of Our God?"[183]

Dom Marmion is too well experienced in spiritual matters to fail to forewarn souls against the frequent and at times opposite dangers which lie in wait for them from the very beginning of the life of union. He writes to a generous soul:

One thing which I must make you notice is that it is often best to let well alone; the uncertain future may be the enemy of the present. Be on your guard that the enemy does not show you things crookedly.[184]

To one tossed about by many interior vicissitudes, he gives this valuable teaching:

Do not be astonished at those alternations of which you are conscious on the surface of your soul; the important thing is that subconsciously, *deep down* in your soul, you are always united with God by intention and love.[185]

It is a mark of wisdom also to know one's weaknesses and failings, the price of humility. Dom Marmion wishes above all—and this is one of the characteristics of his doctrine—that progress in union with God be made constantly in an atmosphere of absolute sincerity in regard to oneself. He writes to a contemplative nun:

* The only way of knowing the state of our soul is by the fruits, "By their fruits you shall know them."[186] Now be quite at peace; I don't in the least look on you as a saint or a very spiritual person, but Our Lord has preserved you pure and free from great sin, and I know He wants to have you very intimately united with Him, "I confess to Thee, O Father... because Thou

hast hidden these things from the wise and prudent, and hast revealed them to little ones."[187] You are one of these little ones.[188]

Writing to a Carmelite nun:

Your inconstancy ought not to alarm you, but inspire you to keep very near to Him Who is all your strength. He loves to see that we are making efforts to be pleasing to Him, even when these efforts are not always as happy as we would have them.[189]

He tells a Benedictine nun:

It is not an illusion to think that one has the desire to belong entirely to Our Lord, even when one has failings at the same time. Even if we happened to fail fifty times a day, we must still each time get back immediately to Our Lord and make acts of love. The desire to love is already an act of love.[190]

To correct yourself of vanity, of the desire to please men, of self-consciousness, the best means is:

1. To do everything directly to please God. The more you look at God, the less you will look at yourself;

2. To thank God, Who is the source of all good, for all the good you do, for your successes, etc.;

3. Not to be astonished, nor troubled, when you happen to fall into imperfections, but to ask forgiveness and, immediately, *sursum corda,* lift up your heart.[191]

Advice of great value, thus developed:

I have been thinking very much of all you wrote to me, and I see that Our Lord is on the way to forming you.

Nothing is more fatal in the spiritual life than the thought that we can do anything good without Our Lord, and our self-love is so subtle, that *unconsciously* we attribute to ourselves the little good that we do, which spoils everything. Our Lord, out of love, leaves us sometimes to our wicked nature, and then we are frightened in seeing all the evil and the possibilities of evil hidden in us. It is not that we are worse than before, but Our Lord lets us see the depths of evil which grace had covered. During these moments, we should act in union with God's designs, by humbling ourselves profoundly and throwing ourselves into God's arms.

The devil tries to trouble you by his subtleties, so that you may cease to act well for fear of acting from vanity. We must never cease doing well for that reason, but quietly purify our intention. The best way is to unite it with Jesus Christ, and *with His intentions*, and if there is anything imperfect in your intentions this union with Jesus Christ will heal it.

Next, your revolts and repugnances come in great part from your physical state. At those moments when one cannot pray it is better to work, etc. We will speak again of all this at my next visit.[192]

This doctrine at once very supernatural and very human, very lofty and marked with Benedictine discretion, actuates all Dom Marmion's direction. We have met with it in one of his earliest letters:

As for what regards the desire for perfection, you ought to seek it with *all the ardor of your soul*, but at the same time resign yourself to walk at the rate that Our Lord wills for the moment.[193]

We shall find it again, nearly thirty years later, in a letter written to a Benedictine nun a few months before his death:

I have a great longing to make of you a little saint, I see that Our Lord desires it. What He asks is that you do ALL FOR LOVE, quite simply. And don't be astonished if you are not always as perfect as you might wish.[194]

2. *The Spirit of Detachment*

Perfect union with the Infinite is something ineffable, and, however intense may be the desire to attain to it, all is of no avail without inmost detachment from all things and patient submission to God's good pleasure.

In his spiritual works, above all in *Christ, the Ideal of the Monk,* Dom Marmion has so much insisted on the active mortification of the senses and the mind that we need not go back on the subject; he has shown at some length the primary necessity of the voluntary successive spoliations which constitute the *reliquimus omnia* ("we have left all things"), and prelude to union with Christ: *Et secuti sumus te* ("and have followed Thee").[195] Compunction of heart, the manifold forms of renunciation and penance, the detachment of poverty, the abasements of humility, the total destruction of the natural "self" in its deepest psychological depths by "the constant labor of obedience"[196]—that whole course of voluntary immolation he sets before us in its full extent, opening widely the royal way of the holy cross for those who will walk in it. The life of union is first of all tributary to a long and faithful effort in asceticism.

What is further brought out in his letters is the no less imperious necessity for purifications which the soul ought bravely to accept from God's own hand, before attaining to perfect union with Infinite Purity. For, in this work which is to culminate in the communion of the human with the divine in the plenitude of charity, God Himself intervenes to render the soul capable of such union. Dom Marmion is not unaware of this; we shall see that under his pen neither the ideal of union nor the holy exigencies it requires are lessened; but we shall see too with what sureness he leads souls and with what invincible confidence his unwearying goodness knows how to inspire them. He will not hurry over the different stages, but he will be there, at every turn of the way, at every crossroad, to warn and guide.

Before the dark night into which God makes the soul enter, nature shudders. A true drama begins, a moving drama, often a wholly interior drama, having for witnesses—and sometimes for actors—only heaven and hell, and whereof the stake is nothing else than the sanctity of the soul. In these cases it is not enough for the soul, however generous, to collect her forces and gather up her energies: she wants an enlightened, sure and resolute guide who will lead, embolden, sustain, in case of need uplift her, defend her sometimes against herself, and ever draw her on until she comes at last to the lofty goal which the Lord wills for her.

The most essential renunciation is the renunciation of sin; Dom Marmion sets forth this doctrine in terms at once clear and encouraging:

You must be persuaded that your sinful past is in no way an obstacle to very close union with God. God forgives, and His forgiveness is Divine. With the Angels, God was not merciful because they had no miseries. With us, who are full of miseries, God is infinitely merciful. "The earth is full of the mercy of the Lord."[197]

And what might appear astonishing, but is however very true, is that our miseries entitle us to God's mercy.

What you lack, what leaves some feebleness, some want of equilibrium and stability to your spiritual life, is not having practiced the virtue of penance enough. Confession remits every sin, but there remains in the soul, as it were, the scars of sin which a contrary habit—the virtue of compunction—should eliminate.

I want you therefore for a few years to give yourself to the virtue of penance. In doing so you must not remember your past life in detail but recall that you have offended God and constantly regret it. The virtue of penance will be manifested in you by these three things:

1. *The spirit of compunction.* I very much want you to keep always in this spirit. Say often, "O God, be merciful to me a sinner."[198] By this prayer we say nothing, we simply show God our misery; we feel that we are only poor sinners in His sight.

You certainly should not lay your mind under restraint and forbid yourself all acts of praise and thanksgiving, but compunction should dominate. Often make the Stations of the Cross; always begin your prayer by casting yourself as a sinner at God's feet. I am sure that if you thus steep yourself in compunction during some years until God calls you to another state of mind you will derive from it immense good for your soul. If you have delayed giving yourself to Our Lord, well! repair that by giving yourself to Him now without reserve, with great fidelity and great generosity. And never fear that your past faults and infidelities will prevent you reaching the degree of union that God intends for you; in an instant He can repair all that.

2. *Mortification.* For you it will consist above all in the perfect observance of the Rule and the regular discipline, and in the mortification of the common life generously accepted.

3. *Love.* You ought to love much; you have a loving heart capable of loving much. You must repair the past by great love for Our Lord. You must love like Mary Magdalen at Jesus' feet, "Many sins are forgiven her, because she hath loved much." Say often to Our Lord, "My God, I want to love Thee to a far greater degree than I have offended Thee in the past."[199]

The same law of renunciation remains no less necessary for souls purified from sin:

I don't forget you. I pray for you with all my heart. As it is with the earth so with the garden of our souls there is a winter that comes before the springtime. It is necessary.[200]

I rejoice that you have quite decided to refuse nothing to Our Lord Who, certainly, is calling you to great union with Him. To arrive at this union, we must pass through many sorrows and trials and above all that of feeling how weak we are in ourselves.[201]

He writes to a contemplative nun:

* Be faithful and you will arrive at great union. It is impossible, dear child, to arrive at intimate union with a crucified Love, without feeling at times the thorns and nails. It is this which causes the union. You must not be discouraged if Our Lord lets you see a *little* of your misery. He bears with it always... hides it from you, but you must see and feel it, before it comes out. This is painful and humiliating for a little Irish woman![202]

And in a letter to a married woman:

Our perfect rest is Paradise. Here below we must stay near Jesus, and upon earth, Jesus presents Himself above all upon the cross. That is His official portrait. He gives us little joys so that we may be able to endure life and merit our heaven, but He blends a portion of the cross with them. He will *certainly* give you the grace to manage your affairs if you confide yourself to His Love. Don't think too much of the future. Live in the present. The future will bring its own grace when the trial comes.[203]

Detachment from created things is particularly important. In laying down the principles of this detachment, Dom Marmion finds excellent and happy turns of speech to be borne in mind:

Ask for nothing, refuse nothing, desire nothing except what God desires for you, that is to say your perfection. All the rest is not *He Himself*. One thing is necessary: It is He.[204]

* Place *all* your consolation in God, not in the sense that you should reject all other joy, but that no human consolation should be *necessary* for your peace.[205]

He writes to a contemplative nun:

Imitate above all your patroness in her inviolable fidelity to Him Whom she had chosen as the one and only Bridegroom of her soul. Oh! yes, I dream of you as so perfect! I picture you arrived at the point when no fiber of your heart will any longer vibrate save at contact with Jesus, when no creature, *in so far as it is a creature*, will be able to attract, rejoice or sadden you. We have not got there yet, neither you nor I. But we desire it "from the depth of the heart,"[206] do we not? Then Jesus will be the Master of our soul, for as it is true that "whosoever committeth sin is the slave of sin,"[207] so it is likewise true to say, all proportion guarded, "whosoever loveth the creature is the slave of the creature."[208]

In another letter to the same, he indicates the deep-lying reason for this detachment:

I am loath to offer you stereotyped good wishes for your feast. Every day I place my desires for your sanctification in the Heart of the Divine Master and I ask Him to render you more and more "consecrated" to Him. "Christ" means consecrated, anointed, living for the Father:[209] separated from profane things and altogether vowed to God. That is the divine ideal we should realize by our *consecration* on the day of our profession, and by our *daily consecration* on the altar with Him. The consecrated chalice may be employed only to contain the Precious Blood. The consecrated virgin exists only for her Divine Bridegroom and has no right to employ her person or her faculties except for Him; all is consecrated, reserved to Him.[210]

The widest field of renunciation, one of supreme efficacy for the soul, is offered by the trials willed or permitted by God Himself:

Blosius, a *great* Benedictine mystic, says that the best form of mortification is to accept with all our heart, in spite of our repugnance, all that God sends or permits, good and evil, joy and suffering. I try to do this. Let us try to do it together, and to help one another to reach that absolute abandonment into the hands of God.[211]

He writes to a nun:

Keep your soul set at large and act with the holy liberty of the children of God Who has taken possession of your soul, and if you abandon yourself without reserve to His Wisdom and Love, He will send you many mortifications far better than any you could choose for yourself.[212]

A precious grace is that of patience in the midst of trials:

When a soul is yielded up to Jesus, out of love and without reserve, He takes her, He keeps her near His Heart, and by a Providence full of divine wisdom and love, He provides her with a thousand occasions of practicing patience. Now *patience hath a perfect work*.[213] Patience perfects our soul, for, as Saint Benedict says: "It is by patience that we share in the sufferings of Christ."[214]

On this important point of Christian asceticism, we have the good fortune to possess several groups of Dom Marmion's letters covering a period of thirty years. It has seemed preferable, in this case, to publish them in their chronological order. The continuity of thought will thus be the better emphasized.

The first extracts are taken from letters written in 1894 and 1895 to a young girl who aspired to enter the cloister. The way that leads to divine union is narrow and arduous. Dom Marmion sets forth this general law by taking care to maintain the vigor and clearness of the Gospel:

May Our Lord take you *all* to Himself and give you courage to endure the trials so necessary for those who wish to be united to the Crucified. Here below Our Lord presents Himself to us upon the cross; the crucifix is His official image, and union with Him is impossible if we do not wish to feel the nails that pierce Him through.[215]

Dom Marmion knows by experience that nothing gives impetus to the soul like the humble and loving looking upon Jesus. It is the Paschal season and the Liturgy has brought round the reading of the episode of the disciples of Emmaus. After expressing his good wishes for Easter, he adds:

You remember Jesus' words to the two disciples whom He walked with on the road to Emmaus. "Ought not Christ to have suffered these things, and so to enter into His glory?" We are His members and it is impossible for us to enter into His glory without having suffered with Him. The more one is united with Jesus Christ, the more one lives by His life, and this life here below is a life of suffering. Saint Paul says, "We have not a High Priest who cannot have compassion on our infirmities: but One tempted in all things like as we are, without sin." Look at His holy Mother. No one ever suffered as she did, for no one has ever been so united with Him as she was. And to yearn for union with Jesus, is to yearn for suffering.

So, courage! you are on the right road, and one day you will understand this more clearly.[216]

And on another occasion:

As for you, my child God leaves you your little miseries. You have need of them:

1. To keep you in that abasement where you often find yourself and where the Good God will always seek you;

2. That you may glorify Jesus acting in you and that you may not attribute to yourself the little good you might think you do of yourself.

And here is the beautiful development he gives of this thought. It could not be clearer or more persuasive:

For what regards your weaknesses, your failings, the Good God permits them in order to keep you in humility and in the sense of your nothingness. God can always draw good from our miseries, and when you have been unfaithful and have failed in confidence and abandon to His holy will, if you humble yourself deeply, you will lose nothing but, on the contrary, you will advance in virtue and in the love of God.

If everything happened to you just as you could wish, if you were always in robust health, if all your exercises of devotion were performed to your satisfaction, if you had no doubts or uncertainties for the future, etc., with your character you would quickly become full of self-sufficiency and secret pride; and instead of exciting the bounty of the Father of Mercies and of drawing down His compassion on His poor weak creature, you would be an abomination in God's eyes. "Every proud man is an abomination to the Lord."[217] You must therefore set to work. Our Lord loves you, He sees into the depths of your soul, even into recesses hidden from yourself, and He knows what you need; leave Him to act, and don't try to make Our Lord follow your way of seeing things, but follow His in all simplicity.

Uncertainty, anguish, disgust are very bitter remedies necessary to the health of your soul. There is only one road that leads to Jesus, namely that of Calvary; and whosoever will not follow Jesus upon this road must give up the thought of divine union. "If any man will come after Me, let him deny himself, and take up his cross, and follow Me."

Take courage! I have as much need myself of these considerations as you have, for nature does not like sacrifice, but the reward of sacrifice namely, the love of God, is so great, that we ought to be ready to bear yet more in order to attain to it.[218]

A little later, Dom Marmion shows his spiritual daughter the reason of these purifications and directs her gaze to the Divine Model:

You have given yourself entirely to Our Lord and He has

taken you at your word. It is not a small thing to give oneself unconditionally to Our Lord. He sees right down to the bottom of our heart. He sees within miseries, weaknesses, the possibility of falls which you do not suspect, and in His infinite mercy and wisdom, He makes you follow a treatment which produces great results in your soul, although it is bitter to the taste. You must never look back, but abandon yourself absolutely into God's hands. It is impossible to arrive at intimate union with Our Lord without passing through these interior trials. So don't be discouraged in feeling such a great repugnance to suffering. Our Lord Himself felt this same repugnance, and the Holy Spirit inspired the Evangelists to describe to us at length this terrible agony of Our Lord in the Garden of Olives, so that those who are sorely tried may be consoled by the sight of their God overwhelmed with sorrow and weariness. This is why Saint Paul tells us "We have not a High Priest Who cannot have compassion on our infirmities: but one tempted in all things like as we are, without sin."

So have good courage! I tell you in the name of God that you are in the right path, and that in suffering with patience and love, you are glorifying Our Lord and doing His holy will at present.[219]

The divine goad continues its painful work in the soul. But in this mystery of purifying suffering, the most delicate love is revealed:

I feel the greatest compassion for you in the trial that the Good God is sending you at this present moment. It is a martyrdom. However I am entirely conformed to the holy will of our dear Lord Who sends you this cross from His inmost Sacred Heart. Believe me, and I say this to you on the part of God, this trial has been sent to you by the love of Our Lord, and it is to do a work in your soul that nothing else could have done.

It will be the destruction of self-love, and when you come forth from this trial you will be a thousand times dearer to the Sacred Heart than before. So although I feel great pity for you, I would not for anything in the world have it otherwise, because I see that Jesus, Who loves you with a love a thousand times greater than that with which you love yourself, permits this trial to befall you. You may be sure that during all this time I shall recommend you to the Good God in my prayers and sacrifices, asking Him to give you the strength to profit greatly by this grace.[220]

All along such a path as this, many temptations lie in wait for the soul; of these none is more dangerous than that of losing courage beneath the burden of the day and the aridity of the road:

You know that God chooses to lead us along the path of perfection by the light of obedience, and often He deprives us of all other light and leads us without letting us understand His ways. During this kind of trial you must keep yourself in complete submission and have an unshaken confidence—despite all that the devil or your reason may suggest to the contrary—that He will know how to draw His glory and your spiritual advantage from it in quite a different way from that which you would have chosen for yourself. I tell you in the name of God that this trial is a *great grace* for you, and I am so convinced of it that as soon as I saw its beginning I knew that it would continue some time; it is most painful, it is the greatest cross that God can lay upon the soul He loves, but as long as you are obedient, there is no danger.

The only real danger for you at present would be to yield to the temptation to discouragement. Every cloud has a silver lining and after a storm comes a calm. And I am sure that when this trial has done its work in your soul, it will cease and you will enjoy such peace and union with God as you have never

known. One of the principal results that God intends for you by
sending you this cross is an ABSOLUTE *resignation and submission*
to His holy will. Try to place yourself in this disposition and
that will hasten the end of the trial.[221]

———⚬∞∞⚬———

**Another young girl had long aspired to give herself entirely to God
in the contemplative life; when, after many obstacles her desire was
about to be realized she became the object of mortifying
reproaches. Dom Marmion writes to her:**

The hour of sacrifice has struck. You already feel that it is
not a small thing to aspire to the dignity of being the bride of
the Crucified. Already He is associating you with His sufferings
and ignominies. Herod treated Him, Eternal Wisdom, as a fool;
Pilate treated Him as a seducer, the people preferred Barabbas
to Him. And you, who aspire to very close union with Him, are
beginning to be scorned and misunderstood by this world which
would have surrounded you with adulation if you had chosen to
smile upon it. Take courage, my child, these are certain signs
that Our Lord wishes to unite you very closely to Himself and
to associate you with the works which He does for His Father's
glory. Better to stay in the world than to bury yourself in the
cloister if you are not prepared to be a victim. Better to become
a Sister of Charity or a hospital nurse than a Carmelite, if you
do not wish to remain with Mary at the foot of the Cross to
share the agony and shame of your Divine Bridegroom. What if
people do treat you as selfish or ungrateful—(I too have gone
through all that)— let it suffice that Jesus sees your heart.[222]

**At last she enters Carmel and in the peace of the cloister is
sheltered from the world's contemptuous sarcasms. But let her not
be lulled by illusions, nor content herself with mere words. To
enter this cloister is to enter the lists where she must sustain great**

combats in the cause of the Most High; the palm is only to be won at the price of the most generous fidelity:

I see more and more that what Jesus Christ wants of you is that you abandon yourself without reserve to His will and His love. Place no reservation, no condition to doing this, for He only gives Himself entirely to those who give themselves to Him without counting the cost.

But, my dear daughter, don't be under any illusion. It is much easier to *say* to Our Lord, "I give myself to You without reserve" than to do so in reality. There are very few, even among His spouses, who love Him *for Himself*. The greater number love themselves more than they love Jesus, for it suffices for Him to impose something upon them that upsets their customary plans or goes against their inclinations for them to want no more of Him. The generosity with which a Carmelite makes her novitiate is of *great* value. Consider it as a great evil, a great fault to say to Our Lord, "Lord, I know that You desire this from me; I know that it would be more pleasing to You for me to do this, but I do not consent to do it." For when one allows oneself to say "No" to Our Lord, to bargain with Him, that perfect understanding, that mutual abandon which constitutes real union between the Bridegroom and the bride becomes impossible.

Let her not fear however; Jesus is there. By the aid of His all-powerful grace, He will support her upward efforts:

Be convinced, my child, that Jesus will never impose a sacrifice upon those who yield themselves up to Him, without giving them a generous measure of the necessary grace and help to carry the cross, and without carrying more than the greater part of it Himself. To doubt this would be doubt the love and fidelity of Jesus Christ, it would wound Him to the depth of His Heart.[223]

In the course of the way the guide becomes more urgent:

I have a great longing to see you become a true daughter of Saint Teresa, with a *great* heart, detached and *free* from every creature, above the geegaws which captivate the hearts of so many women. Jesus wants to reign in your heart without rival or competitor. He wants to give Himself *without reserve* and, for that, He exacts unconditional surrender before the rights of His Infinite Love, His Divine Beauty. We will work at this, will we not, my child, cost what it may.[224]

The hour of religious profession, the hour when solemn promises are exchanged forever, arrives. Dom Marmion wishes, he says, to leave a "little souvenir" to the one under his direction. In reality he traces out for her a program of the highest perfection. It is impossible to curtail these pages of such high and supernatural inspiration. Noble and austere language which a disciple of Saint John of the Cross might comprehend:

My vow of poverty prevents my offering you a little gift for the great day of your profession, but Holy Scripture assures us that *Verbum bonum super donum optimum.* "A good word is better than a gift."[225] I am going then, my daughter, to leave you a little souvenir that later on may serve to remind you of the thoughts and affections that the Divine Spouse will inspire you with on the day of your mystical nuptials.

When I look at your soul in the light of prayer, I see that Our Lord has led you by the hand, has protected you against the dangers and seductions of the world, and by an altogether gratuitous love has called you to the religious state that He may find in you a faithful spouse wholly yielded up to His love and His holy will.

Our Lord is Master of His gifts and, *without any merit on their part,* He calls certain souls to more intimate union with Him, to share His sorrows and sufferings for the glory of His Father and the salvation of souls, "I fill up those things that are wanting of the sufferings of Christ, in my flesh, for His body, which is the Church."[226] "We are the body of Christ, member for member."[227] God could have saved men without them having to suffer or to merit, as He does in the case of little children who die after baptism. But by a decree of His adorable wisdom, He had decided that the world's salvation should depend upon an expiation of which His Son Jesus should undergo *the greater part* but in which His members should be associated. Many men neglect to supply their share of suffering *accepted* in union with Jesus Christ, and of prayers and good works.

That is why Our Lord chooses certain souls to be associated with Him in the great work of the Redemption. There are elect souls, victims of expiation and praise. These are dear to Jesus beyond all one can imagine. His delight is to be in them. Now, my dear daughter, I am convinced that you are one of these souls. Without any merit on your part, Jesus has chosen you. If you are faithful, you will attain close union with Our Lord, and once united to Him, lost in Him, your life will bear much fruit for His glory and the salvation of souls. On the day of your mystical nuptials one sees only the flowers of the crown that Jesus places upon your head. But, my daughter, never forget that *the spouse of a Crucified God is a victim*. I say this to you, for I foresee that you will suffer, and you have need of much courage, much faith, much confidence. There are deserts to be traversed, you must pass through darkness and obscurity, days when you feel powerless and forsaken. Without that, your love would never be deep nor strong. But if you are faithful and abandoned to Him, Jesus will always hold you by the hand. "Though I should walk in the midst of the shadow of death, I will fear no evils, for Thou art with me."

And here is the admirable conclusion:

So, my dear daughter, give yourself without stinting, yield yourself up without fear. Do not *ask* for suffering, but *yield yourself up* to the wisdom and love of your Spouse that He may operate in you all that the interests of His glory demand. He will come to you every day in the Holy Sacrament *in order to change you into Himself.* Let this eucharistic life of Jesus be a continual model for you. There, Jesus is a Victim immolated to the glory of His Father, and given over as food to His brethren, even to those who receive Him with coldness and ingratitude, or to those who outrage Him. You, too, my daughter, be every day more and more a *victim* immolated *to the glory* of the Blessed Trinity in prayer, Divine Office, and mortification, and a *victim of charity* immolated to souls by expiation, and to your sisters by patience, kindness, indulgence. Be a *great soul* who forgets herself to think of the interests of Jesus and of souls. Do not be stayed by the trifles which occupy the thoughts and the life of so many consecrated souls. Let us help one another to arrive at this sublime ideal which I desire for myself as I do for you.[228]

The director's predictions were to be realized. This soul was to be given over to the action of the strong God to the powerful hand of that Spouse "Who," according to Bossuet's expression, "breaks the bones in order to reign alone."[229] But how intimate and deep the union that results from this! Dom Marmion then writes a page of rare elevation of thought as also of exquisite delicacy of feeling:

Jesus has chosen you for His spouse. "You have not chosen Me, but I have chosen you." His design in thus choosing you was to unite you so intimately with Himself, to render you so perfectly His spouse, that you might no longer live save for Him. That is why He has drawn you by the attractions of His love, not to an active order (where however your impetuous nature would have served you well) but to Carmel in order that you may live unknown and hidden with Him, a *true* spouse, *finding all her happiness in her Beloved*, seeking *nothing* apart from His good pleasure and the interests of His glory.

This vocation, my daughter, is *very great*, "all hidden with Christ in God." A faithful Carmelite who lives only for Jesus and for His members does more for souls in a few months than others do in a lifetime. For she enters to such a degree into the intimacy of her omnipotent Spouse that she disposes of all the treasures of His Heart, and these treasures are infinite!

But all this on condition that she fulfils her role of spouse with perfect fidelity and great perfection. *She has only that*, and if she does not give that she does less than a Sister of Charity or a nurse, for they, although they do not remain always near the Bridegroom, occupy themselves with His members. In a kingdom, the Sovereign has his ministers, his generals, his devoted servants; he loves and appreciates them, and they do much for him and his people. But his bride, if she be faithful and loving, is dearer to him than the whole of his Kingdom and her least desires are commands for his heart. But if she is not faithful, if her smiles are for others, if the Sovereign sees that she does not find *all* in his affection, if he sees that *she has need* of other loves, other affections to make her happy, she does not fulfill her role as spouse, he does not find his delight in her heart, and he is better pleased to be with his ministers, his faithful servants.[230]

Oh! my daughter, how I long to see you belong altogether to Jesus, how I pray, how I implore Our Lord to make you worthy of your magnificent vocation! How I desire to see you a holy Carmelite! For that, it is necessary to *immolate* nature, never to follow it, but to place every fiber of your being in the hands of your Spouse, so that nothing may stir in you except at His command and love. Jesus is ever in your heart; lay down your *whole* being at His feet a hundred times a day, leaving to Him the full disposal of everything. And then, when He takes you at your word, when He cuts into the living flesh, shudder, yes, but kiss the hand of God Who is preparing you for divine union with the Crucified. "I am the true Vine; and My Father is the Husbandman... everyone that beareth fruit in Me, My Father will prune and cut away all that is imperfect in him that he may bring forth more fruit."[231] Saint John of the Cross says, "Once we have given ourselves to Jesus in religion, we ought, in a spirit of faith, to look upon each member of the Community as being charged by Jesus Christ to try us and to form us."[232]

However the dark night is prolonged; the path by which the soul ascends is not only arid but it seems to her to be interminable. She needs a firm as well as gentle hand to draw her on towards the heights where the Sacred sign of the *Sponsus sanguinis* (bridegroom of blood)[233] dominates. With what delicacy Dom Marmion devotes himself to this task! Could more human and at the same time loftier expression be found?

I have *seen* that you have been suffering, I have suffered with you. We are so much *one*! Yet I could not have wished it otherwise. I have placed you with Jesus like His *Amen* deep in the Father's bosom. He loves you infinitely more and infinitely better than I do. I yield you up to Him as Mary yielded up Jesus, and if He wills to fasten you on the cross with your Spouse, if He wills for you shame, suffering, and misunderstanding, if He wills for you even *immolation*, I will it too as I will it for myself. We are not made for enjoyment down here, our happiness is on high, *sursum corda*. In the Divine plan all good comes from Calvary, from suffering. Saint John of the Cross says that Our Lord scarcely ever gives the gift of contemplation and perfect union except to those who have labored *much*, suffered much for Him. Now my ambition for you is this perfect union, so fruitful for the Church and souls. Saint Paul tells us, "Gladly therefore will

I glory in my infirmities, THAT the POWER of Christ may dwell in me."[234] I wish to see you quite weak in yourself but filled with the *power of Christ*. Jesus has promised that through Holy Communion not only shall we abide in Him but also that *He will abide in us*. That is the *power of Christ*. The more our life flows from Him, the more we have the *power of Christ*—the more it glorifies the Father. "In this is My Father glorified, *that* YOU BRING FORTH VERY MUCH FRUIT; he that abideth in Me, and I in him, the same beareth much fruit."[235]

<hr />

About the same year (1903-1905) Dom Marmion had to occupy himself with a girl little more than a child who, stricken with an implacable disease, was to die after two years of suffering.[236] He wrote her several letters. The elevation of view, the sense of adaptation and depth here revealed make of this collection a real little treasure. We give these extracts in their chronological order:

April 3, 1903.—This life is certainly full of sadness and tears, for we have constantly to see those we love suffer and to be separated from those who are dearest to us.[237] But there is a fatherland on high, the Home of our Heavenly Father. In that land there will be no tears, no separation, there we shall be forever with those we love. But for that, we must suffer here below, and this is why the greatest friends of God suffer much upon this earth so that they may not be attached to the things of this world since they will have *infinite* happiness for all eternity.

Look at Jesus and Mary. They were dearer to God than all mankind, and yet no man ever suffered as Jesus did, and Mary the Mother of Sorrows suffered as never any other mother suffered.

January 29, 1904.—You tell me, my dear child, that sometimes you find it easy to meditate and to pray to Jesus, and at other times you feel no sense of devotion. That is because in the life of the soul as in that of nature there is both summer and winter. We need the summer to encourage us and help us to endure the winter; and we need the winter to teach us that of ourselves we can do nothing and that we depend on God and His grace. Don't be astonished then to feel these alternations which are necessary in the inner life, and try to show God that you serve Him out of love by being as faithful in drynesses as in consolations. These drynesses are often a little warning on God's part to correct us for some infidelity.

May 29, 1904.—The dearer one is to God, the more one suffers in this world. Jesus, God's beloved Son, suffered as man has never suffered. Mary, our Mother, is the Mother of Sorrows. Why? Because God is so good, He gives to unbelievers and to the wicked who will not have the happiness of enjoying His beautiful Paradise, the good things of this world, things which will last a few years and then pass away forever. But to His friends He gives *eternal* good things, for each little suffering borne for God and in union with Jesus will have an *ineffable* reward for all eternity. That is why Mary was so poor; that is why she suffered martyrdom all her life, ever after the holy man Simeon foretold to her the sufferings of her Son.

Try then, my dear child, to unite all your sufferings of body and of *heart* to the Sacred Heart of Jesus, for it is this union which gives all their merit.

October 1, 1904.—You must not be surprised if in your present state of languor you do not always feel that fervor and ardor in your prayers that you would like to have. The poor soul depends so much on the body that when the latter is suffering or languishing it cannot do much. Even the great Saint Teresa, despite her ardor and generosity, bitterly complained that her physical weakness hindered her soul from rising to God in prayer. When we bear this state patiently we are much more pleasing to God and nearer His Heart than when we are full of fervor and consolation, for then our love is pure and disinterested.

October 8, 1904——I was very grieved on hearing you were so weak and suffering, or as you yourself say, so like a little flower drooping upon its stalk. I beg Our Lord daily to give you the courage to suffer, to bear this painful state, for His love and in union with His faintness and weariness and sufferings during His Passion. Yes, indeed, my child, to suffer with Jesus is true happiness, if we could only understand this, for one who suffers is so near His Sacred Heart! But you must often lovingly unite yourself with Him and accept *with Him* and *for Him* all that the Good God wills to lay upon you.

December 30, 1904.——You have been so *suffering*. If there were only this poor world with its trials, separations and sorrows, I should be very grieved at this news, for I love my dear child. But I keep my eyes fixed on that beautiful Paradise where we shall all be one day and where each day of suffering here below endured *with Jesus* and *for Him* will have an eternal reward, joy and rest. Yes, my dear child, Jesus is treating you as He treated His Mother, and as He treats those whom He especially loves. Courage then! I pray daily for you that Our Lord may give you *entire* submission to His holy Will... A single day of weakness and illness borne joyfully for Jesus counts as months [in ordinary health].

February 13, 1905.——If there were not an eternity of rest and joy with God after the weariness, sorrows and sufferings of this life, I should be quite sad in thinking of what my dear daughter is suffering. But I raise my thoughts to that beautiful Paradise where we shall be altogether, forever, with God. Each day, each hour, each instant of suffering borne with Jesus and out of love will be a new heaven for all eternity, a new glory rendered to Jesus forever. In Heaven, Jesus ever bears His five Wounds which are like five suns of dazzling glory, ever proclaiming all He has suffered for love of His Father and for us. And each suffering that *we* shall have endured in union with Him will also be like a sun proclaiming to all heaven all that we have suffered for Jesus.

I pray several times every day for you and your dear parents, that God may give you the grace to adore His ways and to submit yourself with all your heart to the trials He sends you.

March 27, 1905.—The good Jesus will not take it amiss if I write a little word to you during Lent since He has said that what we do to His suffering members we do to Himself.[238]

I am told that you have received Extreme Unction. Your whole body was sanctified and consecrated to God by this Sacrament, and you were placed in His fatherly Hands that He may guard and console you. The grace of this Sacrament lasts during all the illness, and obtains fresh graces for you at each instant.

My dear child, it is very painful and very hard for *nature* to be thus, at your age, so suffering, so powerless. And yet, if one could see you as the angels see you, how one would envy you! Having been baptized and having received Holy Communion, you are the image of Jesus Christ, and now that you are stretched upon your bed of suffering, you are the image of Jesus Christ upon the Cross. Every time you unite yourself to Our Lord Crucified by acts of patience and conformity to God's holy will, you become dearer and dearer to the Heart of Jesus. Your state of suffering accepted lovingly and in union with

Jesus Christ is as pleasing to God as that of a nun, and if you are faithful, if you lose none of the graces you are receiving at present, you may even surpass your sister, in spite of her alpargates and Carmelite togue.[239]

The final thought, so deeply supernatural, is one to be borne in mind: it sums up the great doctrine of Christian suffering:

To endure your sufferings, your state of languor, peacefully and gently, in union with the sufferings of Jesus, is *to do* much.

It is above all by union with Christ Suffering that patience in trials produces its highest results. One would expect this point of doctrine to be set in striking relief by the author of *Christ the Life of the Soul*. Whether he speaks to contemplative nuns, to missionaries or to married persons he retains the same elevated and winning, human and supernatural language. A deep sense of tender devotion fills all these pages. He writes to a Mother Superior:

* Our life is pleasing to God exactly according to the measure in which we are united to the Word by love and resignation. The Sacred Humanity of Jesus gave special glory to God during His weakness at the hour of His Passion. *Deus qui in assumptae carnis infirmitate jacentem mundum erexisti...* "O God, Who didst raise up the fallen world by the weakness of Thy human nature taken for us."[240]

Our Divine Savior associates each of His elect with one of the *states* that He sanctified and deified in His Divine Person. Some are united to His Childhood, others to His Hidden Life, others again to His Apostolic Life, finally, others to His Passion. Some are united to *the weakness* of His Agony, and these give Him the greatest glory.

In our activity, we are so inclined to *substitute* our natural human activity for God's action! But when God throws us down, despoils us of *our* activity, He takes entire possession of us and deifies all the activity which springs from Him. That is what God is doing for you. Your prayer should be to be buried deeper and deeper each day in this Divine will. Place your heart in that of Jesus and let Him will for you. I ask God daily to give you the grace to carry the cross that He lays upon your shoulders. Blosius says that a soul that gives herself without reserve to God, permitting Him to work in her as He pleases, does more for God in a few hours, and, for certain souls, in an hour, than others do by their activity during long years.[241]

From letters addressed to a missionary nun in the tropics we take two admirable extracts of great doctrinal depth and rare elevation of thought:

There is no heavier cross here below than that state of exhaustion and lassitude produced by the climate and by the life you have to lead. But, believe me, there is nothing that brings about the true divine life within us like *union with the weakness of Jesus*.

In espousing our nature in the Incarnation, He took upon Himself all our weaknesses, all our powerlessness, all our sufferings; He made them His own: "Surely He hath borne our iniquities and carried our sorrows."[242] At the time of the Incarnation the Word did not assume a glorious body, like that of Thabor, not an impassible body like that of the Resurrection, but a body made in the likeness of sinful flesh,[243] like to ours in all things, save personal sin. In taking our sins, He uplifted and rendered our weaknesses *divine*, and thenceforth they cry out in us to the Father, like those of Jesus Christ Himself.

It is by *pure* faith, by love without any feeling that this is brought about and, in place of our weaknesses we receive *the strength of Christ in an immense degree*.

And after having once more quoted Saint Paul, he concludes:

I want so much to teach you this great truth and to help you to put it into practice. To do so, you must give yourself up unconditionally to Jesus Christ by accepting in *pure faith* all that He sends or permits. Know, my daughter, that in a soul like yours, which has left all for Him, which in reality seeks only Him, there is an *unconscious* prayer, unfelt but very real, which rises up to God in the midst of your sense of failure, for our desires are true prayers for Him "Who searcheth the reins and hearts."[244] "Your ear has graciously heard the need of the poor."[245] But, for this, the great virtue for you must be *patience*. "Patience is NECESSARY for you."[246] It is by patience, the absence of any, even inward, murmuring, by meeting every trouble with a smile, that Jesus makes you share in His Passion.[247]

A thought which ought to aid and encourage you is that all that God does for us proceeds from His mercy. God builds an eternal monument to His mercy in Heaven.[248] The stones of this monument are *the miserable* who draw down mercy by their misery. For mercy is goodness in face of misery. The foundation stone of this monument is Christ Who has espoused all our miseries. "Surely he hath borne our infirmities and carried our sorrows."[249] He deifies them and gives them an immense merit and value in His Father's sight. If every morning you unite your fatigues, your weariness, your sufferings of every kind with those of Jesus Christ He *will take them upon Himself* and make them His own. As our Blessed Father Saint Benedict says, "It is through PATIENCE that we SHARE in the sufferings of Christ."[250] In patiently suffering the sorrows and fatigues of life we share in the Passion of Jesus Christ. Then, His strength, His virtue, reign in us. "Gladly therefore will I glory in my infirmities, that the power of Christ may dwell in me."

Oh! my dear child, it is a *great grace* to understand this and to follow Jesus in His faintness and weariness. Nothing can draw down divine favors and mercies more than this *patient* union of our sufferings and weaknesses with those of Jesus.

As subject of examen, take the *patient and loving acceptance* of the trials and sufferings of your life. In this way your life will become a continual *crying out* to the Heart of the Heavenly Father.[251]

A lofty doctrine and yet a simply Christian one and most efficacious. This is why Dom Marmion is no less ready to set it before persons living in the bonds of marriage:

It is impossible to go to Heaven by any other way than that which Jesus went by, the way of the cross. You will meet with this cross daily in one manner or another. The great thing is to accept it *in union with Jesus.* For it is that which gives it all its merit.

My daughter, I pray for you every day, that as the days succeed one another you may become more and more dear to Our Lord.[252]

This life is not given by God as a Paradise. It is a time of trial followed by an eternity of joy and rest. Christ suffered all His life, for the shadow of the cross ever hung over Him, and those who love Him share His cross to some extent all their life long. The contrarieties, the misunderstandings, the sufferings of heart and body, household difficulties, all these things form the portion of your cross, and when you accept these trials they become holy and divine by their union with those of Jesus Christ. The virtue that I want to find in you on our next meeting is above all *patience.* Patience unites us exceedingly with Jesus suffering, as Mary was united with Jesus at the foot of the cross.[253]

A few weeks later he wrote these lines of delicate feeling to the same person, as a conclusion to his good wishes for Christmas:

May God bless you for having endured for His love, the pains, the lassitude and cares of motherhood in order to give Him souls to praise Him for all eternity. Mary will bless you because you have shared with her the divine maternity. Saint Bede tells us that each time we teach a soul to know and love Jesus, we beget Christ within it. You will thus be mother of your dear children by a twofold claim.[254]

As always, Dom Marmion directs the soul's gaze on the Suffering Christ in Whom alone is found the principle of patience. The following letter is likewise addressed to a person in the world:

It is quite normal that you should feel forsaken and in a state of dryness and tedium from time to time. All souls that aspire to union with Jesus Christ must pass through that. This sense of incapacity, of weakness, of tedium is needful in order that our pride may not attribute to ourselves what comes to us from God. The sense of almost unconscious peace that you feel in the depth of your heart is a sign of the presence of the Holy Spirit in the depth of your soul.

Jesus is *the Lamb of God* and His immolation consists in this that He *yielded* Himself up like a gentle lamb to all the sufferings that His Father willed to permit for Him. He did not turn His face away from those who spat upon Him. He did not open His mouth. If we wish to be united to this Divine Lamb, we must yield ourselves up in *bare faith* to God's hand that strikes us, to all the sufferings that His love and wisdom permit. That is the best and highest of immolations. Jesus has known weariness, fear, fatigue. He understands all that.[255]

He writes to the same correspondent:

You must penetrate yourself with this truth. All that God

does for us is the effect of *His Mercy*. Misery brought face to face with goodness produces mercy, that is to say it renders the heart of goodness miserable until it has relieved us. We are *miserable creatures* and our miseries joined to those of Jesus cry out to our Heavenly Father. That is a continual prayer provided that we accept the sufferings, the fatigues, the vexations of every moment with patience and resignation. "It is by patience," says Saint Benedict, "that we share in the sufferings of Christ."[256]

And finally, a few weeks before his death, like an ultimate echo of this doctrine so familiar to him, he writes:

* You are on the right road to God, a road which ever leads to Him despite our weakness. It is the road of *duty accomplished through love* despite obstacles. Jesus is our strength. *Our weakness assumed by Him* becomes *divine weakness,* and it is stronger than all the strength of man: "The weakness of God is stronger than men."[257] This is a great, but profound truth. Our dear Lord's Passion is nothing else than this triumph of Divine weakness over all the strength and wickedness of men. But for this we require great patience and the loving acceptance of God's will at every moment. For: "It is by patience that we share in His sufferings."[258] Think well over this in prayer and you will make great progress.[259]

On the same date, November 21, 1922, Dom Marmion wrote the following words to a young girl: they perfectly sum up the whole doctrine set forth thus far; the conclusion is especially to be borne in mind:

* Union with Jesus is *consummated* in *faith*: "I will espouse thee to Me forever."[260] The *sense* of union with Him is His gift, but not Himself. We must leave it to His Wisdom and Love to give or withhold it. We can do nothing without Him, "Without Me you can do *nothing*." This perfect detachment from creatures

and adhesion to Him must come from His grace, and is the recompense of humble prayer and patience. When Dame Gertrude More (descendant of Bl. Thomas More) was dying, her director Fr. Baker, OSB, who had done so *much* for her, came to see her. The Abbess told her he was there. She said, "I need no man." Jesus was all to her. Of course this is very perfect, and we must not fly till our wings are strong enough. Perfect patience under all that God *permits* unites us to Christ's Passion. Try to *smile lovingly* at every manifestation of God's will.[261]

CHAPTER IV

GROWING IN UNION WITH GOD
THROUGH THE PRACTICE OF THE
THEOLOGICAL VIRTUES

1. *Faith*

The life of union with God is, in substance, but the life of grace received at Baptism and given full scope to blossom in a soul purified from sin and detached from self.

The development of this life is wrought, above all, by the practice of the three theological virtues of faith, hope and charity. Through grace, we are radically united to God; by the virtues, which are the faculties, the powers of action, we become capable of making the life of union a practical reality.

Faith makes us to know God. By *hope* we live in the confidence and desire of possessing Him. *Charity* closely unites us to Him in a friendship of benevolence, reciprocity of sentiments and community of life. These three virtues are the specific virtues of the life of union with God; being constantly exercised, they inevitably grow and increase till they come to perfection.

Faith alone is the proximate and proportionate means which can unite the soul to God, for faith has so intimate a connection with God that the act of faith and the act of beatific vision bear upon the same object, although they attain to it in a different way. The greater the faith, the greater is the possibility of that intense union which is wrought by charity.[262]

Pure faith, bare faith, how often Dom Marmion approached this subject! And with what delight, what mastery too! He never wearied of extolling this essentially supernatural virtue, this light infused into the soul by God, the Author and End of the order of grace, this light which makes us participate in God's very knowledge.

It is by the spirit raised by grace and enlightened by the *lumen gloriae* that we enter into contact with God and into possession of Him in Heaven, and it is by the same spirit enlightened by the light of faith that we possess Him here below.[263]

In accordance with the Council of Trent, Dom Marmion has magnificently shown that faith is the root of all justification, the foundation of the whole Christian life. He often comments on those words of Saint Paul, "The just man liveth by faith."[264] When he sets forth the mysteries of Jesus, it is always upon this virtue that he insists, because it puts us in vital contact of grace with Christ, the Son of God. Dom Marmion is never so true to himself as when on this ground.[265] And when he has to guide and encourage souls in this way, he has but to speak out of the abundance of his heart. He writes to a Carmelite nun:

God will give Himself to you with ineffable love in the splendor of the Beatific Vision *during all eternity*, and His glory demands that we serve Him here below as well as we possibly can *in the darkness of faith*. Faith is the supernatural life. It is by faith that the just man lives!

By the Providence of His Eternal Wisdom, God has decreed that our trial here below should be made in faith. We must love and embrace this holy will. If God, in His goodness, grants us from time to time spiritual lights and consolations we ought to accept them with humility; if not, we must serve Him all our life long in *naked* faith, as Jesus naked upon the cross loved and served His Father.[266]

He writes to another nun:

* Go on quietly, living by *pure faith,* without any feeling. Jesus is your supplement in all things, so in your communications with God, if you find yourself dry and "rationalistic," just close the eyes of your soul, and in humble adoration just say one long *Amen* to all that Jesus is doing and saying in your name *in sinu Patris* [in the bosom of the Father].[267]

What does he mean by this pure faith? He is going to tell us and at the same time to extol its greatness and power:

* I am sure God wishes to lead your soul by the path of *pure* faith, that is by faith without any of the self-satisfaction which sentiments and perceived certainty give. From time to time you will receive a ray of light and warmth, and you must live on that, holding on to your faith without any *reflex* consolation, though ever with a very real, but unfelt joy in the depths of your soul. Try to love this way of pure faith, it is so sure, so un-selfish, so very glorious to God. God never gives virtue in a high degree without our having fought and suffered for it. This is true of faith which is the "root and foundation of all justice." You will seem to yourself at times to have almost lost your faith and yet it remains whole and entire in the *fine point* of your soul, all gathered up into so sharp and imperceptible a point that it seems no longer to exist. Close your eyes, and remain with Jesus, saying a loving Amen to all He is gazing at in His Father.[268]

As he has just insinuated, this virtue is difficult to practice: essentially supernatural, transporting the soul into a heavenly Kingdom which "cometh not with observation," it is too often

counteracted by the "impressions" of nature. Dom Marmion often drew attention to this important point; he would have the life of union with God to be sincere, well-balanced, stable:

* You should try more and more to walk by faith and not by *impression*. God has given us our reason, and He wishes us to guide ourselves by that faculty enlightened by faith. It is by reason we differ from animals, and God is glorified by our acting according to the nature He has given us. There are so many, especially women, who form for themselves a conscience of impressions which changes with every wind.[269]

I cannot recommend you too strongly, in your spiritual life, not to occupy yourself with what you feel, with what you experience, you can so easily deceive yourself! A woman, too often, thinks with her heart and judges according to her impressions. You must live by faith.[270]

He writes to a troubled man:

Laugh at your impressions. To yield to them would be a misfortune for you. God wants us to go to Him *by faith*, without impressions, or in spite of them. We must despise them, for they do not count with God.[271]

When you look at Christ upon the cross, do not depend *too much* on what this image may seem to say to you; walk by *pure* faith. If however Our Lord helps you in this way, have no scruple.[272]

The life of faith is above all necessary at the moment of Communion, the preeminent mystery of faith:

As for Holy Communion, my child, it must never be given up. It is the mystery of *faith* and Our Lord often leaves us without zest or feeling so that our *pure* faith may become more robust. In Communion, Jesus works in the spiritual part of our soul, far from the senses, and He produces grace and virtue of which we are unaware.[273]

Your letter has greatly consoled me, for I see that Our Lord is leading you by the true path. Holy Communion being *the mystery of faith*, it often happens to the most fervent to find themselves destitute of feeling and given up to Our Lord in *nakedness* of pure faith.[274]

With advice, he blends kindly encouragement:

Our relations with God are founded upon *faith* and not upon *feeling*; we can be very near to God—and often we are so—and we *feel* very miserable and perverse.[275]

I want your soul to be in peace and your heart set at large in the holy liberty of the children of God. Your heart ought to be so much one with the Divine Heart that His sentiments are yours and that you see only through His eyes. Now the gaze of Jesus is always fixed upon the face of the Father, and He assures us that this Father loves us so much that He has given us the Son of His dilection. Let your life be more and more a life of faith, not a life of impression. Now faith is to believe what Jesus beholds. He is "the author and finisher of faith." I pray for you with all my heart that He may thus be so.[276]

He writes admirably to another nun:

* Believe me, my dear child, Our Lord wishes to be *everything* for you; that is why He allows you to be so *little in yourself*. Try and assimilate Saint Paul's magnificent theology. It is just what your soul wants. You are a "capacity" at present almost empty, and Our Lord wants to fill it.[277]

This life of pure faith is indeed so pleasing to God that it becomes the well-spring of abundant graces and most precious favors for the soul:

I thank Our Lord for the good dispositions He has put in your heart. As long as you remain very little, but full of confidence in Him, He will never fail to shower His favors upon you. You will not always *feel* His presence, but then go to Him by *pure* faith which will greatly please Him.[278]

I am convinced that Our Lord loves you *very much* and that He deprives you of the *sense* of union with Him, because He wills to treat you as a "valiant woman" who walks by faith, not following her impressions as most women do. The log will blaze up one day; for the *desire* to love God, when it is sincere, is so pleasing to Our Lord that He never fails to satisfy it, and that beyond our aspirations.[279]

I see that you go *straight* to God by a loyal and *simple love*. That is the way for you. Our dear Lord wants you for Himself, and for Him alone. He calls you to His mysterious espousals in FAITH. He wants you as spouse so that you may give yourself up to Him and let Him be the Master and Spouse of your whole being.[280]

Therefore he was very happy to be able to render this testimony one day after long years of direction:

I have guided you by this sure path of faith, and I know that although Our Lord has united you with Him to a high degree, it is true however to say of you: *Sponsabo te mihi in fide,*[281] that it is in faith He has espoused you.[282]

Like every virtue, faith has its particularly crucifying trials. Dom Marmion encourages the soul to remain "faithful":

You are passing through a winter, but it is that you may reach a greater union. For the moment remain *united* with Jesus by *faith*: I will espouse thee in faith, says the Spouse.

But faith has its darkness as well as its light, and God is as good when He presents Himself in the darkness of faith as when He appears upon the Thabor of consolation.[283]

From the grievous crucible into which God casts the soul, virtue emerges purer and more powerful. Sometimes too, these trials are interspersed by interior lights which make the soul penetrate into hitherto unknown depths of the mysteries of faith, whilst the hunger and longing for the Supreme Good are intensified within her. Everything seems to combine to baffle and bewilder her.

Dom Marmion knew how to discern the character of those states, those fluctuations, so frequent in this period of spiritual ascension before that abiding peace which fixes the whole being in God is attained. His words bring light, assurance and strength to those who ask him for enlightenment and counsel; he sets before them the figure of Christ, the one and only model of all perfection, the source of all strength, He whose power of attraction is infinite:

God wants of you great poverty and *nudity* of spirit; it is the spirit of Carmel. Jesus stripped of *everything*, separated from everything, lifted upon the cross and living and dying for His Father, there is your model. The more God unites you to Him, the more your whole life will be Jesus Christ—the greater too will be your poverty and your suffering at the moments when God withdraws Himself.

But is not this "poverty" glorious for God and fruitful for the Church?

The soul immolated to God in the nudity of pure faith, of hope and perfect union does more for the Church in an hour than others (more mediocre and less generous) do in their whole life.[284]

Because these temptations against faith are particularly painful, it is necessary to reassure the soul that is grappling with them:

* You are passing through one of those terrible trials through which every soul called to close union with Jesus must pass. "Because you were pleasing to God," said the Angel to Tobias, "it was necessary that temptation should try you."[285] My child, we cannot go to God but through union with Jesus. "I am the way—*no one* goeth to the Father but through Me." Now Jesus went to His Father by passing through Gethsemane and Calvary, and every soul united to Him must pass by the same way.

These temptations against faith are a real crucifixion, and yet you really *do* believe, but unconsciously, and that is why your love subsists and seems to go ahead of your faith. The devil is doing his best to cast you into despair, for he sees that you will one day be very closely united with Him Whom he hates, hence he casts darkness and trouble into your soul, and revolt perhaps in your senses, but this is the path by which all interior souls must pass, if they are to reach perfect union. Blessed is the man who suffers temptation, says Saint James, for when he has been tried, he will receive the crown of life.

Dom Marmion goes on to cite the examples of Saint Hugh bishop of Grenoble, tempted to blasphemy, of Saint Jane Chantal and Saint Vincent de Paul tried in their faith; he recalls the example of Saint Catherine of Siena who after being molested with violent temptations, said to Jesus, "Lord, where were You," and Christ answered, "I was in the center of your heart, sustaining you all the time." Then Dom Marmion adds:

And so it is with you: Jesus *is* in the center of your heart, it is He who causes you to long for Him, so be in peace.[286]

On another occasion he writes these remarkably clear-cut lines. Those familiar with ascetical and mystical questions will recognize in them sure knowledge joined to wide experience:

* I have read your letter attentively in the presence of God, and am quite convinced that you are called by God to a high union with Him. Your present state of soul bears all the marks of one of those interior trials or passive purifications through which the soul *must* pass before attaining to union with *Infinite Purity*.

The Holy Ghost says, "Blessed is the man who is tempted," and Saint James adds "Beloved, be filled with great joy when you pass through various temptations."

Those against Faith and Hope are the most distressing, and a real agony, but *most* salutary. The secret *subconscious* longing for God is *a sure sign* of the presence of the Holy Ghost in your soul, it is a vision of God's beauty in the darkness of faith, but just as the beatific vision which the soul of Jesus *always* enjoyed, did not diminish His agony, nor prevent His soul being sad even unto death, so with yours. It is your purgatory, and Our Lord is holding your soul in those flames until all selfishness and self-seeking are burned out. Then you will enter into the ineffable grandeur of God.

The *very nature* of the trial through which you are passing is the terrible uncertainty it leaves in the soul as to her state. She *seems* to herself to have lost faith and love for she *feels* nothing. It is pure naked faith. This longing for God is a most powerful and constant prayer; for God reads the inmost thoughts of our hearts; and this thirst for Him is a way to His Father's Heart. "Thy ear hath heard *the desire of the poor*," and no one is poorer than those who are serving God in the trials of pure faith.

So now courage! You are on the right road and all you require is *great* patience and absolute confidence in Our Lord's loving care. You are very dear to Him though you may imagine the contrary. He wants you to see for yourself how really miserable and unworthy you are, and that it is His sheer mercy which thus clasps you to His Heart. During all eternity God will give Himself to you in the full and unremitting blaze of His beauty. Here below His glory requires that He be served *in faith*. Let us try and serve Him in faith, just as if we gazed on Him in vision.

Again he refers—and very appositely—to what Blosius says; he recalls how Saint Chantal was long tormented by temptations against faith and "yet received a special gift of Faith and contemplation from God." Then he concludes:

In practice adore God profoundly; then tell Him you accept *all* He has revealed *on His Word alone*, and as the Church speaks in His name you accept Her voice and teaching as His. Make then acts of love, even though you feel nothing.[287]

Thus, little by little, proceeds the divine work of those painful purifications which make faith more vigorous and the soul more deeply humble.

Sometimes, however, the storm of trial ceases and a flash of light breaks through the thick darkness through which the soul is struggling. The guide rejoices when this happens, for he still sees in this the work of God, and he himself is a father. Nevertheless, he knows no standing still; but, always with gentleness, he brings the soul back to the truth which sets free.

* I was so pleased to receive your letter and to see that Our dear Lord had lifted the veil a moment, just as He did for the disciples [on Mount Thabor]. Of course we must walk not by vision but by *faith*. Yet He condescends to our weakness and from time to time allows the light of His Divine mercy and beauty to pierce the clouds and darkness in which He habitually

envelops Himself, "clouds and darkness are round about Him."[288] You have come down from the mountain on which you would have dwelt forever. "Lord, it is good for us to be here."[289] And you now see "only Jesus."

My dear child, *you* must never forget that in the present order of providence God is glorified by our *faith*: "Without faith it is impossible to please God."[290] He from time to time gives us to *feel* that He is sweet, and that He loves us, but this is the exception, and He expects us to believe and confide in His love without any feeling of it, *nos credidimus caritati Dei,* says Saint John, "we have believed in God's love for us."[291]

In the psalm *Attendite*,[292] God is ever complaining that, despite the repeated *proof* of His ever-loving providence, the Jews were ever falling back into distrust. "They were not MINDFUL of the multitude of His mercies,"[293] and so He complains of them, "they always err in heart."[294]

Now, my dear child, I have studied your soul in prayer, and I *know* that God wants you to serve Him by pure faith in spite of all sorts of repugnance; and so you must be satisfied to go on in faith without consolation, nor feeling, trusting in Him, and in the words of His minister, who speaks in His name. He will often leave you in your weakness and seem to deprive you of every help, and yet He is ever in the center of your heart, guiding and protecting you. You must have a great faith, not only in His *love*, but also in the *wisdom* of His guidance.[295]

These lights of the Holy Ghost which shine fugitively but powerfully upon the deepest mysteries often result, as we have said, in intensifying the soul's hunger and longing for God:

* That hunger for Jesus and for His love is a *continual* prayer; Our Lord keeps you dry and hungry just to excite the longing, which is so pleasing to Him. You are all right. *Your* way is *faith,*

faith without feeling—faith made strong in the weakness of temptation and doubt. You must accept your *way*. It is He Who chose it for you.[296]

In other lines, Dom Marmion describes this state more at length but with no less precision:

* Our Lord is leading you by the way which is most glorious for His Father, and most advantageous for you. The way of *pure faith*. God intends giving Himself wholly and without reserve in the full blaze of His light to you in perfect love *for all eternity*. Here below His glory requires that we love and serve Him in faith. He gives us consolations and light to help us to go on in the darkness, but these are not essential; and when He sees a soul *decided* to love and serve Him despite all, He tries her by leaving her in darkness without feeling or special lights.

In reality there is a deep but invisible light in the inmost recesses of her soul. It is this invisible light which gives her the longing for God. This *longing* is a most efficacious prayer, and an homage to God's beauty. Saint Francis de Sales says we ought to be satisfied with God's way of leading us and not expect "particularities." God loves to see a soul content to go on in the way He leads her.[297]

He writes to a nun:

* The light and interior movement you received during the retreat were verily from God and a grace. When such graces pass, they are often followed by seasons of doubt. Saint Teresa even after moments of highest union, during which she was incapable of doubting the Divine action, frequently fell back into doubt and trouble when the Divine contact had ceased. Of course in your case there was no question of such exalted favors, but I mention the fact in order to show you that doubt may succeed to absolute certitude in such cases.[298]

The same valuable advice as to confidence is instilled in the following lines:

* There is *no illusion* in the conviction of intimate union you experience at times, though when it is past you may begin to doubt its reality. Our life is a life of faith, and experimental conviction if continued *might* diminish the merit of faith. There can never be any illusion in the desire of uniting your will *perfectly* with the Divine Will. You cannot practice this too much. Saint Jane Chantal wrote that for years her prayer consisted "en laissant sa volonté *s'enfoncer* de plus en plus dans la divine volonté."[†] C'est là votre voie.[‡] I pray for you daily, and feel Our Lord will show forth His mercy once more in lifting up your nothingness to His perfect union.[299]

2. *Hope*

Faith reveals to man the greatness of his destiny, namely, eternal participation in the Divine life begun even down here by a life of intimate union with God. It is a destiny exceeding the exigencies, the rights and the powers of nature, but which faith helps the faithful soul to attain. God has put within us, together with the light of faith the impetus of hope, an inmost conviction of attaining this beatitude in spite of obstacles, a constant desire of coming to it in relying upon God's omnipotent aid, His promises, and, above all, upon Christ's merits. That is Christian hope. A necessarily arduous virtue the practice of which is often subject to many a hard test. Dom Marmion has some magnificent pages on this subject.

Here we see in what terms he sums up the whole doctrine on hope and shows the greatness of this virtue.

[†] *En laissant sa volonté*...: "in allowing her will to *sink* more and more into the Divine will."

[‡] *C'est là votre voie*: "This is your way."

To a person in the world:

In the measure we approach God through Jesus Christ we approach the light for "God is light, and in Him there is no darkness."[300] Now this light produces two effects:

1. It reveals to us the greatness of our God. His love, His perfections.

2. It also reveals to us the abyss of misery, of pettiness, the possibilities of sin and betrayal, hidden in the depth of our heart.

This is the great prayer of Saint Augustine: "May I know Thee, O my God, may I know myself." The knowledge of one does not go without the other.

When God discovers to us the abyss of our misery, it needs all the strength of the Holy Spirit, all our confidence in the love of our Heavenly Father, all our faith in the Blood of Jesus Christ in order not to be crushed by the weight of our weakness, and yet what glorifies God is when, in the full knowledge of our misery, we persist in hoping in His love.[301]

What Dom Marmion especially delights to put in strong relief is that all God's work in regard to humanity is a work of mercy.

For some time past God has been making me see in a magnificent light that His Majesty's whole plan, His whole "economy" towards us is an economy of *mercy*. It is our miseries which, united to Christ's sufferings and infirmities, draw down all the graces He gives us.[302]

He says again:

God has been giving me for some time past a strong light, and this light is shed over my whole life. When God looks upon this poor world, upon this multitude of the miserable, incredulous and sinful, what does He feel? "I have compassion on the multitude."[303] Our miseries excite His mercy. Not only that, but as we, through our baptism, are members of Christ, our miseries are His. He has taken them all upon Him. He has assumed them and rendered them divine, and the Father, in looking upon our miseries and weaknesses, sees those of His Son which cry out to Him for mercy. "Blessed is he that understandeth concerning the needy and the poor."[304]

Therefore the sight of our miseries ought not to be a subject of astonishment or discouragement for us:

The abyss of our miseries is very great, greater even than we think. But God's mercy is infinite like God Himself. If we lay open our soul to Him with all its infirmities and sins, His Divine gaze penetrates this abyss of which we cannot see the bottom. His gaze goes into the most hidden recesses and brings us strength and light. There is only this Divine gaze that is able to penetrate into our inmost being and sound the depth of our woes. God alone too can supply the remedy and we may be assured that He will do so.[305]

He writes to a Carmelite nun:

For you, it is not good to scrutinize the lowest depths of your soul. If during prayer, God throws *His* light into your soul and in this light reveals to you, your misery and baseness, it is a signal grace. But you are not in a state to examine and analyze your soul in a natural light.[306]

And again to the same:

I pray for you continually that you may respond perfectly to the designs of Jesus. It is necessary to realize all your baseness before the final union, but *this baseness must be seen* in God's light. Jesus is all powerful, He can and He will sanctify us.[307]

Dom Marmion often renewed these encouraging words:

Do not be astonished or discouraged at the sight of your imperfections; not being wilful, they draw down the compassion and mercy of our God, Who is touched by the weakness of His children.[308]

He says to a Benedictine nun:

To know how to display our miseries before God is to draw down grace; never forget that. If a soul, even one far advanced in virtue, ceased to regard her own miseries and to take complacency in the gifts she has received, she would infallibly fall. For you, my dear child, learn to say with Saint Paul, "Gladly therefore will I glory in my infirmities, that the power of Christ may dwell in me."[309]

God has His own merciful designs in revealing our misery to us.

At the beginning, God does not show us our misery because it would discourage us; but He reveals it little by little; then we feel that we truly have need of Him.[310]

It is a great mistake to suppose that God is dazzled by our perfection; let us seek rather to draw down His compassion and mercy by acknowledging our miseries.[311]

The knowledge of our misery keeps us humble.

Do not let yourself be discouraged by your miseries; the Good God leaves you some miseries to convince you thoroughly that you can do nothing. He does not wish us to be able to attribute to ourselves whatever good we may accomplish. *Jesus is our holiness*; we must be very faithful and wait for Him to act in us.[312]

As well as being a source of humility, the light of our misery keeps us in the truth:

You are feeling humiliated at seeing that you are worth nothing and can do nothing; that is just what the Good God wants you to see. It is an excellent thing to feel humbled and, believe me, you are much more in the truth now than when you judged yourself to be better.[313]

Here is his excellent conclusion in a letter to a nun:

As long as we live, we shall have our little miseries. Without that we should incurably proud, and that would be the greatest of miseries.

Our Lord sometimes encourages us and sometimes brings us down in order to try us. "The Lord killeth and maketh alive, He bringeth down to hell and bringeth back again."[314] We should imitate Saint Catherine of Siena who, when Satan urged her to vanity, humbled herself beneath the devils' feet and when they tried to make her fall into despair, lifted herself up even to the throne of God by the thought of His mercy.[315]

Dom Marmion well knew how to extol this twofold sense of humility and confidence, virtues which ought to go together and which are only true when thus united. Of all the themes dear to him there is perhaps none developed by him with so much supernatural complacency. Let us draw abundantly from this treasury.

Sometimes he reminds those under his direction of our total dependence in regard to grace:

Occasionally Our Lord takes away sensible grace and leaves us to our own natural weakness, as He did for His Sacred Humanity in the Garden of Olives. We feel then all our misery, our laziness, our selfishness, but He only acts thus in order that we may learn by experience how much we depend upon Him for everything.

Once it was asked of Him, "Who art Thou?" And He answered, *Ego Sum Principium qui et loquor vobis*, "The Beginning, Who also speak unto you."[316] *Principium*, beginning, means "primary source." He is essentially the *Principium* of all good: "Attribute any good that one sees in oneself to God and not to oneself."[317] Now as He is the Truth, He wishes us to be convinced (and to testify to our conviction) that all that is good in us comes from Him alone. The deepest wound dealt to our soul by sin is that of self-love, by which, in practice, we continually attribute to ourselves the good we do. To heal us of this wound, Jesus often allows us to prove what we are without Him, that is to say, nothing. "Without Thy Divine help, there is nothing in man."[318] At such moments we must not be troubled but say with Saint Teresa of Avila, "Lord, behold the fruits of my garden."[319]

* You are just going through what all souls called to close union with the "Crucified" must suffer. God sometimes allows sufferings of all sorts—bad health, weariness, temptation, difficulties etc., to swoop down at once on the soul to purify her. She must *feel* her utter *dependence* on Him. Souls united as yours is with Our Lord, whose whole life comes from Him, suffer more than others when He leaves them. This winter is only to prepare for a more fruitful summer. All you can do is to bow your head and accept the trial, and bear with the Lord till He come back. Jesus gives us the example. In the Garden of Olives it is said "He began to fear, and to be weary, to be heavy and sad." I pray for you with all my heart.[320]

At other times, he fixes the soul's gaze on high, upon God's infinite mercy and the aid of His omnipotence:

The holy Liturgy tells us that God manifests His Almighty power "ESPECIALLY by showing mercy and forebearance."[321] Be for Him a monument of His *mercy* during all eternity. The deeper our misery and unworthiness the greater and more adorable His mercy. The abyss of our misery calls to the abyss of His mercy.[322] It is a great consolation to me to see that you are walking in this way which is so sure, which leads so high and glorifies the Precious Blood of Jesus Christ and the mercy of our God. It is my way too. Help me with your prayers.[323]

Most often the two thoughts are linked together and to this circumstance we owe an admirable page:

* I do feel intense pity for you and pray for you with *all my heart,* as I know what you are going through. No, dear, it is not pride—of course there is pride in us all—but that is not the reason of the awful isolation, and want and hunger for God's love. No, dear, it is God's doing. He is purging your soul in order to prepare it for union with His Divine Son. "If anyone bear fruit, My Father will purge him, that he may bear more fruit." Now I want you to have confidence in me and believe my word. It is not our perfection which is to dazzle God, Who is surrounded by myriads of angels. No, it is our misery, our wretchedness *avowed* which draws down His Mercy. *All* God's dealings with us are a consequence of His *Mercy* (Mercy is Goodness touched by the sight of misery). And that is why the great Saint Paul says, let others go to God leaning on the perfection of their life (as the Pharisee), "for me, I take glory in my infirmities that my strength may be Christ's virtue." If you could only once understand that you are never dearer to God, never glorify Him more than when in the full realization of your misery and unworthiness, you gaze at His *infinite* goodness and cast yourself on His bosom, believing in faith that His Mercy is *infinitely greater* than your *misery.* Saint Paul tells us that God has done all in *laudem et gloriam gratiae suae,* "for the praise and glory of His grace." Now the *triumph* of His grace is when it raises up the miserable and impure and renders them worthy of Divine union. See Mary Magdalen: She was a *sinner by profession,* she had seven devils in her whom Jesus expelled, and yet He not only allowed her to touch His Divine Feet, but it was to her He appeared first on Easter morning. He is a Spouse infinitely rich and powerful, and when He chooses a poor little child like you to be His bride His joy is to enrich her poverty, and clothe her with His own beauty. You are now passing through a period of trial, but Jesus loves you *dearly.* He is so happy to see you *want* to be loved by Him. That is not self-love, it is wishing for what God wants you to wish. If I could only get that into your head, and keep your eyes fixed on Him—on His Goodness—and not on your little self. "Seek the Lord: seek His face constantly."[324]

<hr />

Dom Marmion did not cease to sustain the soul's confidence in God's mercy during times of trial. Should not the master be particularly reassuring at such times?

Nothing is more pleasing to God than unshaken faith and confidence in the midst of darkness. Make a great practice of acts of confidence *even when you feel nothing.* It is just in these moments of dryness and darkness that these acts are most meritorious, the most pleasing to God and the most useful to your soul. Ordinary souls, that have not given themselves without reserve to God, find no difficulty in making acts of love and confidence in God during times of consolation and success, but it is the property of those whom God calls to union, to more intimate familiarity with Himself, to persist in hoping in Him in spite of every appearance which might tend to make them doubt the Divine promises. Such as these say with holy Job, "Although He should kill me, I will trust in Him." They say to God, "My God Thou art my Father, Thy Son Jesus hast said that Thou art our Father, that Thou lovest us, that Thou never refusest anything that we ask in His name. My God, I believe all this, and although the world, the devil and all hell should tell me the contrary, I believe Thy word *simply because Thou hast said it.*" Never forget that faith is the beginning, the progress and the consummation of perfection.[325]

The same tone ten years later:

Your letter was a great joy to me because it was a proof that Our Lord hears the prayers I offer every day for you, and that you are truly on the path that leads to Him. Your desire to imitate the great Saint Paul who says, "I live, now not I; but Christ liveth in me," is exactly what I should have wished, for all true holiness consists in living the life of Jesus Christ.

But for Jesus Christ *alone* to live in us, nature must die, and nature dies with difficulty. Do not be astonished on feeling repugnance and even at times strong temptations; all that is necessary—at least almost always—in order to arrive at perfect union with God. We are led to say "Blessed is he that endureth no temptation," and yet the Holy Spirit says just the contrary, "Blessed is the man that endureth temptation."[326] Temptation makes us feel our weakness, and this knowledge of our weakness is a real power. In the Epistle of last Sunday's Mass,[327] Saint Paul enumerates all the wonderful things he had done and suffered for Jesus Christ and he ends by saying, "Therefore I glory in my infirmities, that the power of Christ may dwell in me." If we could only understand this mystery of our weakness being our strength! In the same way as poor beggars glory in their hideous sores and, far from hiding them, show them in order to attract the compassion of the charitable, so we ought to rejoice in the thought that we can do nothing without Jesus. Tell Him so often and be glad when the opportunity presents itself of feeling the depth of your misery and weakness. "The more you are confounded by the sense of your misery," Our Lord said to Saint Margaret Mary, "the more I stoop down to embrace you in the power of My Love."[328]

What joy for him when he sees a soul, filled with divine light, enter resolutely into the way of confidence. He writes to a Mother Superior:

In your letter there is a phrase which pleases me very much, because I see in it the source of great glory for Our Lord. You say, "There is nothing, absolutely nothing in me upon which I can take a little security. Therefore I do not cease to cast myself with confidence into the heart of my Master." That, my daughter, is the true way, for all that God does for us is *the result of His mercy* which is touched by the avowal of this misery; and a soul that sees her misery and presents it continually to the gaze of Divine Mercy, gives great glory to God by leaving Him the opportunity of communicating His goodness to her. Continue to follow this attraction, and let yourself be led, in the midst of the darkness of trial, to the nuptials of the Lamb to which He destines you.[329]

And again, a few months later, to the same:

Our Lord urges me to pray much for you that you may remain with great generosity on the altar of immolation with Jesus. A soul, even a very miserable one, thus united to Jesus in His agony, but like Abraham, "hoping against hope"[330] gives *immense* glory to God and helps Jesus in His work in the Church.[331]

The merciful and auxiliary power of God is the basis of our hope; the merits of Jesus and our supernatural solidarity with Christ, the Head of the Mystical Body, are its surest and most efficacious support. The great, and so to speak, the sole motive of our confidence in the concrete and living form, is Jesus. Just as He is the great Revelation of the Father, in Whom all revelations are found, Jesus is the sole pledge wherein the Father has reunited all others.

This thought constantly recurs in Dom Marmion's letters, at times in a brief clear-cut form, most often, as we should expect, developed with particular ease.

1904.—To feel one's misery is a very good disposition. If a King wished to take a poor maiden for his bride, she would say to him, "I have nothing; give me the wherewithal to clothe and adorn me." Since Jesus Christ has graciously willed to take you as His bride, rely upon Him. It is Jesus Christ Who is all your treasure.

1908.—If you are miserable, God is *miserator et misericors*, compassionate and merciful.[332] You must throw yourself with confidence into Christ's arms.

November 1, 1908.—In all things lean upon Jesus. Without Him we are nothing in God's sight. He is our *Supplement* in everything.

He writes to a Carmelite nun in 1913:

Jesus living in you is your *All*: "Who of God is made unto us wisdom and justice and sanctification and redemption."[333] He is your Supplement, so much so that when we act in His name, the Father beholds in us only a member of His Son, and our weaknesses are the weaknesses of His Son. From time to time, as it was for Him in the Garden of Olives, He makes us feel all the weight of our burden and of our weaknesses. Then go ahead perfectly abandoning yourself to Jesus Christ.

In the quite latter years of his life, when he drew nearer to the eternal light, Dom Marmion's tone became still more penetrating:

February 8, 1921.—I have the conviction that a woman like you, a faithful wife and the mother of a numerous family is very dear to the Heart of Jesus. He is the faithful Friend Who thoroughly knows all your difficulties and Who, in His love, loves to supply for what is wanting in your actions.

1922.—We are full of miseries, but we have the signal honor of being members of Christ; that is why Our Heavenly Father dotes upon us. Live united to Jesus Christ, and, in Him, yielded up to the Father.

March 31, 1921.—May God bless you and take you all to Himself through the veil—the Sacred Humanity of Jesus. This veil presents to the Father the torn body of the Bridegroom and all He has suffered for the bride.[334]

May 1922.—Jesus assumes your little sufferings to render them Divine and make them His own, "Surely he has borne our infirmities."[335] All that the Father does for us, He does it for His Son Jesus, and in bestowing His gifts upon us, He rewards Jesus in our person, "Blessed is he who understandeth concerning the needy and the poor."[336] The poor, in this case, is Jesus become man for us.

But these brief thoughts, although containing so much, are not enough for him; he lived this doctrine too intensely to fail to disclose to others all its depth and fruitfulness. He writes to a person in the world:

Your soul is in God's hands; He loves it, He looks upon it unceasingly and He makes it pass through the states that, in His Wisdom, He sees to be necessary for it. As the ground has to go through the death of winter and the grain of wheat to die before bearing the fruits of harvest, so your soul needs to go through the wine-press of temptation and weakness that Christ may make it bear His virtue and Divine life. The more understanding we have of our weakness and of that depth of wickedness that lies in our heart, the more we honor God in believing in the greatness of His goodness and mercy.

I see more and more, my dear daughter, that no virtue is solid if not built upon the foundation of compunction and the *true* knowledge of our misery. According to the Divine Plan, God must be glorified by the power of His grace. Those who do not *feel*, who do not *see* their misery, do not know the need they have of grace. Therefore Saint Paul rejoices in the knowledge of his weakness in order that all his strength may come to him from Christ. "I glory in my infirmities, that the power of Christ may dwell in me." That is why the Good God leads us by this path.[337]

Another time it is a complete outline which this master of asceticism sketches out with a few luminous strokes of the pen:

For the moment, I will only give you two or three principles which should be the tenor of *your* spiritual life:

1. God does all things for the glory of His Son Jesus. Now, Jesus is especially glorified by those who, convinced of their extreme incapacity, lean upon Him, and look to Him for light, help, everything.

2. You should try to realize more vividly that being a member of Jesus by your baptism and more and more by each Communion, your needs, your infirmities, your faults are, in a true sense, the needs, the infirmities, the faults of Jesus. "Surely he hath borne our infirmities and carried our sorrows. And the Lord hath laid on him the iniquity of us all."[338] "He made Him to be sin."[339]

3. When you feel your weakness and misery, present yourself fearlessly before the eyes of your Heavenly Father in the name

and in the Person of His Divine Son. "Gladly therefore will I glory in my infirmities, that the power of Christ may dwell in me."[340] The weaker you are, the more our Lord wishes to be your all. "His left hand is under my head, and His right hand shall embrace me."[341]

The texts he has just quoted are favorites with him; on the one from Isaiah he gives a beautiful commentary in the following letter throwing a light on all his teaching. To a person in the world:

* *"Vere languores nostros ipse tulit et dolores nostros ipse portavit,"* Truly hath He borne our infirmities etc. has a very deep meaning.

1. It means that He took all actual deliberate sin on Himself and expiated it in His Person, *Posuit in eo Dominus iniquitatem omnium nostrum,* The Lord hath placed on Him the iniquity of us all.

2. It also means that as Head of the Church, He accepts in our name (His members) all our miseries, our meanness, our infidelities, our sufferings, and suffered from them in our name, and sanctified and deified them in His Person. No pain or suffering or weakness of His members was hidden from Him. He took them *willingly* on Himself.

3. It also means that by thus taking them on Him, He took the sting out of them, and helped us to bear them. Yes, try and love Him alone and all others in and for Him.[342]

I thank you for your little word and I am happy to see that you wish to belong unreservedly to Our Lord. Despite our miseries, or rather because of our miseries, we ought to lean fearlessly upon Him. "Gladly therefore will I glory in my infirmities."[343] I see more and more that when we come before the Heavenly Father as the members of His beloved Son—"now you are the body of Christ, member for member"[344]—the sight of our miseries does but draw down His look of mercy. *Abyssus abyssum invocat.* The abyss of our miseries calls upon the abyss of His mercy. I often think of you before Our Lord, for neither distance nor circumstances can separate that which is united in the love of our God.[345]

And again to a missionary nun he writes these lines full of persuasive power:

We are members of Jesus Christ and so united to Him, having such *solidarity* with Him, that all our sorrows, all our weariness, our heaviness, our trials of body and soul are ASSUMED by Him and unceasingly cry for mercy to the Father. It is His Son, His beloved Son, Whom He sees in us, and His mercy unceasingly inundates us with graces for ourselves and for others. Say from the bottom of your heart "We have believed the love God has in our behalf."[346] I believe in the love of Jesus for me, a love so great that His sufferings and His merits become mine. Oh! how rich we are in Him![347]

In order to illustrate his doctrine in accordance with his usual plan, he contrasts two categories of souls:

* There are two ways of presenting ourselves before God. 1) As the Pharisee of the Gospel, leaning on our own works and asking God to reward us for our justice. "I observe all Your law, I fast, I give alms. You ought to be satisfied with me." God detests such self-righteous people, though they be really very correct and irreproachable. 2) As Saint Paul, "I regard all my own righteousness as dung, my whole confidence is in Jesus Christ Who through His merits gives to my works all their value." Hence he glories, not in his works, but in his infirmities. "Gladly therefore will I glory in my infirmities." Such people are dear to God, because they glorify His Son, and this is His sole desire.

And now for the application:

You are rich in infirmities and were you to lean on Christ alone, doing all, suffering all in His name, united with Him, He would render you more and more agreeable to His Father. He would bring you with Him into that sanctuary which He calls *Sinus Patris,* His Father's bosom, and there, under God's eye, you would constantly try to please Him by doing what you feel is *most* pleasing to Him. Those alone dwell in God's bosom who have an immense confidence in His fatherly goodness and mercy which are infinite, and who try their best to please Him in all things.

Now there is your program for the present... I feel Our Lord has given you to me as my child whom I am to present to Him as one of the triumphs of His mercy, for Saint Paul says, "He hath chosen the weak, and the feeble and the things of nothing that no flesh might glory in His sight."[348]

"The triumph of God's mercy!"—with what beautiful pages this theme has inspired him! He writes to a nun:

* I have been thinking about your soul. Despite your very real defects and misery which are doubtless much greater than what we see, God loves you dearly, and wishes to substitute His greatness to your littleness; His generosity to your meanness; His truth and wisdom to your insufficiency. He can do all that if you only let Him. "I confess to thee, O Father, Lord of Heaven and earth, because thou hast hid these things from the wise and prudent, and hast revealed them to LITTLE ONES." You are one of these very little people whom God deigns to look upon.

Try to look much more at God than at yourself; to *glory* in your miseries; to love virtue more than you fear vice; to glorify the *infinite* merits and virtues of Jesus by drawing from them lovingly to supply your need.

Now, my child, there's a program for a whole year, yea, for a life.[349]

This is quite true; but such is the weakness of human nature that it is necessary constantly to return to these truths, above all when the soul, too preoccupied with her misery, risks sinking into the slough of discouragement. Then the father's voice becomes gently pressing and imperative, so keen are his convictions. Writing to a nun:

* Your last letter almost pained me, for I see that you allow the sight of your miseries—which are very *limited*—to hide the riches which are yours in Jesus Christ, and these are *infinite*. It is a great grace to see our miseries and littleness, which, in reality, are much more extensive than we imagine. But this knowledge is a real poison unless completed by *immense* faith and confidence in the "all-sufficiency" of our dear Lord's merits, riches and virtues which are all ours. *Vos estis corpus Christi et membra de membra.* You are His body and the very members of His members. The members really possess as *their own* all the dignity and merit of the person whose members they are. And this is what glorifies Jesus, namely, to have such a high appreciation of His merits and such a great conviction of *His love in giving them to us* that our misery and unworthiness do not discourage us.[350]

There are two categories of people who give little glory to Jesus Christ:

1. Those who neither see their misery nor realize their unworthiness, and consequently *don't feel their need of Jesus Christ*;

2. Those who see their misery, but have not that strong faith in the Divinity of Jesus Christ which makes them, as it were, happy to be thus weak in order that Jesus may be glorified in them. How far you are from glorifying in your infirmities!

Strive to have a *very pure intention* in all that you do. Unite your intentions to those of your Divine Spouse and do not trouble about the result. God does not give a premium to success.[351]

He wrote a few years later to another nun:

Your very kind letter was a true consolation to me, for nothing gives me so much pleasure as to see my children give themselves to Our Lord without reserve.

Nothing glorifies the Good God so much as a soul who, whilst *seeing* her nothingness and misery, confides in the merits of Jesus Christ and in the Heavenly Father's mercy. Those who do not know their misery believe themselves good and agreeable to God on account of their personal goodness. They do not feel an extreme need of Jesus; they give little glory to God. Jesus is our *all*. He is the complement of our misery, of our poverty, and He gives Himself to those who are "poor in spirit."

I want you to be very bright, to set your heart at large. "I have *run*, O Lord, the way of Thy commandments, when Thou didst *enlarge* my heart." Sadness is a breath of hell; joy is the echo of God's life in us.[352]

One day Dom Columba wrote these profound words:

The whole history of Jesus is the triumph of the power of the Word supporting the weakness of His Humanity.[353]

Is it not also the history of those whom God deigns to call to perfect union with Himself? Is it not in leaning upon the Incarnate Word, His merits and His grace, that they can hope for everything from God? Dom Marmion is constantly saying so:

* What I want to see in you, dear child, is that profound conviction that all our real strength is the strength of Christ. Saint Paul is so anxious that this virtue alone should be the source of his activity that he rejoices in his weakness and takes glory in it. It is this Divine virtue coming to His members from Christ which gives all the beauty to our actions. As the Church prays in one of her collects, we "rely ONLY upon the hope of heavenly grace ALONE."[354]

And later on, in the year preceding his death:

* Look at God through Jesus' eyes... We are the members of Jesus Christ and our miseries assumed by Him, cry out for mercy in His name to the Father,

He is ever before God's face, and hidden in Him. His prayer as He gazes in His Father's face becomes ours.

I understand so well Saint Paul's "Gladly therefore will I glory in my infirmities THAT the power of Christ may dwell in me."[355]

And he sums up his teaching in this emphatic thought, quite in the spirit of Saint Paul, which is to be found at each instant, so to speak, all through his correspondence:

The poorer we are, the more Christ's ineffable riches find their place in us. Our misery, known and avowed, draws down His liberality.[356]

3. *The Self-Surrender of Love*

The practice of the virtues of faith and hope must be sustained and crowned by that of charity, the supreme virtue: "Yet the greatest of these is charity." We have seen above that love is the very principle of union with God.[357] The following pages give us Dom Marmion's teaching on "one of the purest and most absolute forms of love"— the spirit of abandonment.

In *Christ, the Ideal of the Monk*, Dom Marmion has left pages, numbering amongst the most lofty contained in his conferences, on this virtue at once so necessary and so difficult to practice. In his correspondence, having to deal with individual states of soul,

he brings out the more particular aspects of the virtue of self-surrender, and thereby we gain a complete notion of all that this master of asceticism thought on a capital point of the life of union with God.

The objective basis of holy abandonment is the will of God Who ordains all to His glory and to our union with Him. Therefore one cannot attain this virtue unless imbued with a profound spirit of submission:

The virtue which will lead you to the acquisition of all the others is *the spirit of submission*. Keep yourself in the spirit of submission to God. Often unite yourself to the sentiments of obedience that the Heart of Jesus had towards His Father, above all in prayer and Holy Communion. Submit yourself not only to God's commands but to His every good pleasure, to the events which He permits, to all that He arranges for you. This virtue of submission will lead you to true abandon.[358]

This holy abandonment is itself one of the essential conditions of true progress in union with God:

As you so well say, the condition of all progress in the spiritual life is "to deny oneself, in order to follow Christ."[359] But Louis de Blois (whose works I read with delight) says that we have said all there is to say about abnegation when we define it as complete resignation to the Divine Will in all its manifestations and *permissions*. He says that a man perfectly resigned with Jesus Christ to all the Divine Will is very near to God without appearing to be so. For the time being, do with *your whole heart* what God lays upon you by obedience, by remitting yourself entirely to His love and His Providence for the future.[360]

He writes on the same date to a nun:

Those whom God destines to intimate union with Himself ought to put no reserve to their *abandon*. You must throw yourself into His arms with your eyes shut. You must make an act of complete abandonment to God; give yourself to Him, once and for all, without reserve. This condition must be regarded as essential. I understand that such or such thing makes you suffer, but all that is accidental. What is essential is that you belong altogether to God. Consider yourself as God's "thing" and never take yourself back. When you have communicated, tell Our Lord that you accept, like Him, all the Father's will; tell the Father that you wish to belong to Him like this Word that you possess.[361]

Such total and absolute self-surrender to Love is the source of most precious graces of union:

Our Lord is the Master of His gifts, and as He is infinite Wisdom, we go straight to the Father when we rest upon Him.[362]

When a soul yields herself *entirely,* out of love, with closed eyes, to the guidance of Wisdom, of Omnipotence and Love, that is to say to God, "all things work together unto good" for her.[363] Jesus assures us that the Father's love is so tender, so vigilant that not even a hair of our head falls without His permission. That is the way for you; keep in in spite of all the devil may do to get you out of it.[364]

Is not the example of the saints a palpable proof of this?

When one gives oneself over entirely to the Divine direction all events work together for good. Saint Catherine of Siena, if she had followed her inclination, would have stayed all her life alone in her cell, but Our Lord wanted her in the midst of the multitude, of armies, and in relation with Popes; and as in all this, she only obeyed the Divine call, Our Lord kept her always near Him.[365]

God even measures His gifts according to the degree of this spirit of filial abandonment full of confidence and love:

* The more I pray for you I see that your *way* is absolute and unreserved abandon. God will care for you just in so far as you cast yourself and all your cares on the bosom of His Paternal love and providence. When, in His presence, in the darkness of faith, adore Him in His *ways,* in His providence, His often unfathomable wisdom. Then cast yourself on His bosom just as a child. Unless you become as little children, you shall not enter into the Kingdom of heaven.[366] He will treat you as you treat Him and give you that "joy and peace in believing" of which Saint Paul speaks. Offer Him a daily holocaust of all sensitiveness, leaving yourself and all that concerns you in His loving care. "Cast thy care upon the Lord, and He shall sustain thee."[367]

This spirit of abandonment is so high a virtue, and one so glorious for God Whose highest perfections it honors, so advantageous too for the soul, that Dom Marmion never ceases to demand it. Throughout his correspondence, but especially during his latter years, echo the most urgent appeals, the strongest exhortations to this loving abandonment.

December 15, 1894.—There will never be any peace for you except in the *complete abandonment* of yourself in the hands of your Heavenly Father. It is always necessary to come back to this point, for Our Lord requires of you this testimony of your confidence and love. Each time then that you feel troubled and distrustful, you should try *quietly* by prayer and through union with Jesus, to bring your will to this *absolute submission,* to this complete abandonment of yourself, of your future and of everything, into God's hands.

November 20, 1916.—Keep yourself thoroughly at God's disposal. For my part, I offer your soul to Him every day that He may dispose of it according to His Wisdom and Love.

April 12, 1917.—Abandon yourself blindly into the hands of this Heavenly Father Who loves you *better* and *more* than you love yourself.

January 12, 1918.—What is most pleasing to God is *absolute and unreserved abandonment* to His Wisdom and His Love.

October 8, 1920.—Having left all for God, you ought to expect neither happiness nor satisfaction until you are with Him forever. The Good God gives you so *many* tokens of fatherly tenderness and solicitude, that you ought to respond by complete abandonment. Nothing honors God so much as this surrender of oneself into His Hands.

November 20, 1922.—Abandon yourself blindly to Love; He will take care of you despite every difficulty.

December 5, 1922.—Look at everything with *the eye of faith* and in a spirit of *absolute abandon*. God has His designs in all that He ordains and in all that He does and in all *that He permits*. We should render to Him the homage of our confidence. He has written, "Cursed be the man that trusteth in man."[368] "The Lord gave, and the Lord hath taken away: blessed be the name of the Lord."[369]

———— ∞ ————

But it is important in this delicate matter to keep free from illusions. With his customary prudence, the result of long experience of souls, Dom Marmion enlightens us as to the true nature of this spirit of abandonment; reading his grave and precise warnings we do not come across the least trace of quietism even in its most mitigated form:

What gives simplicity and peace to our lives is the sincere and complete abandon of oneself to God for His glory. To abandon ourselves is to give to God all that we are and all that we have in order to be *His thing* of which He can dispose at will.

Jesus says, "Father, all My things are Thine,"[370] and the Father took Him at His word and delivered Him to unheard of torments. Many people speak of abandon, but very few keep their word with God. They give themselves to God to be His property, and as soon as ever God begins to dispose of this property for His Glory and according to the designs of His Wisdom, they cry out, they murmur, and let it be seen that their abandon was not serious, it was only a meaningless word.

And after having quoted a saying of Mother Mary of the Divine Heart (Drosto zu Vischering), he continues:

When we have made our religious profession, we become so much God's "thing," His property, that each time we try to arrange our life, our occupations for ourselves and according to our own views, we are using something that belongs to God and hence comes the loss of His gifts and graces. The chief thing for you is to *scrutinize very closely* the movements of your heart, your motives (of action), this kingdom of God which is within you. All the beauty of the King's daughter is within,[371] and this beauty consists in that perfect simplicity of love which in everything only considers God and His interests.[372]

A difficult virtue is this, for God's ways are not always ours:

When one gives oneself sincerely and without reserve to the Good God He disposes *everything* for our good. There are stages in life which do not seem to us to be advantageous for our soul, but, in reality, they make part of a Divine plan for our spiritual formation. So accept the present situation in a spirit of faith, with great confidence in the goodness of the Heavenly Father, and with great love. For those who love God all turns to their good.[373]

But:

Nothing is more perfect and pleasing to God than thus to abandon oneself to His good pleasure, even and above all when this good pleasure lays the cross upon our shoulders. God loves to choose what is weak and little to carry out His designs, in order *all* may be *divine*.[374]

He writes to a nun:

I am much opposed to setting an ultimatum to God, or requiring His Divine majesty to give us signs or tokens of His will.[375] Far better to go simply by faith, taking counsel from those who have mission of guiding us. The best thing would be to make a novena to know the Divine will, asking at the same time for a cure if that enters into God's designs. But do not make this cure a condition. It may be that your sufferings are a part of the divine largesse.[376]

He says in a letter to one of his monks:

I can write you *only a word*. I will say to you with Our Lord, "Thou art careful, and art troubled about many things; but one thing is necessary,"[377] namely to abandon yourself with filial confidence into the hands of the Heavenly Father and of the one who represents Him. "For those who love God, all things work together for good..." *The best* of all preparations for the priesthood is to live each day with love, wherever obedience and Providence place us.[378]

Those who really wish to live in a spirit of abandonment must expect purifying trials:

When a soul gives herself for love's sake and without reserve to Jesus, He takes her, He keeps her near His Heart and, by a providence full of Divine wisdom and love, He provides her with a thousand opportunities of practicing patience. Now "patience perfects the soul."[379] As our Blessed Father says, "it is by patience that we share in the sufferings of Christ."[380]

It is particularly at times of spiritual aridity, of interior darkness, that the exercise of this virtue becomes difficult and painful. On these occasions the guide, in the person of Dom Marmion, shows himself full of compassion, helping the soul to respond generously to the solicitations from above. As we have already stated more than once, his delicate forethought ever tempered his most supernatural exigencies:

 * The time approaches when you must leave X... and go where God calls you.... I want you like Abraham to put yourself in God's hands *absolutely*. Every time that God called Abraham, his invariable answer was "Here I am!" No explanations, no plans. The *Lord* calls and the servant obeys. I want you to choose a day on which you wish to make your offering of self to God's loving providence; let me know the day and I shall offer Holy Mass for you and place you on the paten with Jesus, so that your oblation may be agreeable to the Father. The more I gaze at God through the eyes of Jesus living in my heart, the more clearly I see that nothing can be so high, so divine as to remit oneself totally to God. Surely the Creator has a right to dispose of the creature whom He has drawn from nothing; surely He in His infinite wisdom knows what we are best suited to accomplish in His plan; surely His infinite love is the most secure resting-place for our blindness and weakness.[381]

I pity you with all my heart in your interior trial. I know what it is by experience. It is *very painful*. Sometimes God leads us to the edge of the precipice; it seems to us we are on the point of uttering hateful blasphemies. It is the devil working on the *surface* of the soul! Jesus Himself was given over to the devil's fury. "This is your hour and the POWER OF DARKNESS."[382] From that moment the heart and soul of Jesus were the object of hell's terrible attacks. "Surely he hath borne our infirmities."[383] Nothing purifies the soul like this inmost trial. It prepares for Divine union. Then the strength of Christ becomes the soul's only strength.[384]

In another circumstance, he borrows a pleasing comparison from Saint Francis de Sales. Writing to a nun:

* On reading your letter, I saw that your soul is passing through the fire of *love in darkness*. Saint Francis de Sales paints your state perfectly, while describing his own during the last years of his life. A prince had a musician who was most devoted to him. His joy was to rejoice the heart of his prince by his beauteous singing and the sweet harmony of his music. However at the same time, he himself took a vast pleasure in listening to his melodies. At last he became absolutely deaf. He could no longer find any pleasure *for himself* in his music and chant, but he continued to play and to sing with *all his heart* just to give pleasure to his beloved prince.

This is your case. I know your heart, and I know that you love God dearly, but just as Jesus on the cross, He alone must see and feel the fragrance of that love. You must be immolated in the darkness of this Calvary. Take this as *certain*.[385]

To exhortations, he joins prayer. He writes to a Carmelite nun:

I know you are to such a degree in God's arms that I can wish nothing better for you than the perfect accomplishment of His holy will in you. I pray much for you, but solely that you may lend yourself without reserve to God's action.[386]

And several days later:

I love your soul as I do my own and I pray Our Lord to guide you in all things according to His holy and adorable will and to provide you with every opportunity of letting Him act freely in you, for that is your way.[387]

A trial particularly dreaded by those seeking God is to believe themselves to be separated from Him and to feel their powerlessness to find Him. Abandonment is the only refuge of the soul in her helplessness. Writing to a nun:

* Your soul is very dear to God, but He wants a more perfect *abandon* into His hands, and allows you to feel all your impotence, as long as you fail to look for all things from Him.

Your present state is due in part to physical weakness and in part it is a trial; when it is past, you will find that you had been getting nearer God, though it seemed you were drifting from Him.

The sign that your present state is not due principally to your infidelities—though of course it is likely they are not wholly foreign to it—is that you feel deep down in your soul a great want of God, which is a real torment, as you seem so hopelessly estranged from Him. It is He who gives this double and seemingly contradictory sentiment, He wants you to *long* for Him, and at the same time to *see* that of yourself you are quite incapable of finding Him. He will come in the end, "The Lord hath heard the desire of the poor."[388] You are one of these poor ones just now.[389]

Subjected to such variations, the soul should remain firm and confident; nothing is more glorious to God:

* You must not pay too much attention to the fluctuations which are ever passing over the *surface* of your soul. Like the sea, it is constantly ruffled, but in its depths it is all God's. Ask the Holy Ghost to give you an abundance of His gift of *Fortitude*. Nothing so honors God as to lean on Him in full confidence, just when we feel weak and incapable, "When I am weak, it is then that I am strong... I glory in my infirmities that *His strength* dwell in me." (Saint Paul.) May you be filled with Christ's strength. The spouse is never so pleasing to her beloved as when she bears all her weight on the strong arm of her beloved.[390]

Let the soul then persevere generously in this way despite the trials the Lord permits: the hour will come when she will be filled with peace in the most intimate union with God:

When Our Lord wishes to unite a soul very closely to Him, He makes her pass through many trials. But if this soul remits herself without reserve into His hands, He arranges *everything* for her greatest good, according to Saint Paul's words, "All things work together for good to them that love God." God's glory demands that we hope in Him in difficult circumstances. To hope in God, to rest upon His bosom when things go well is not a lofty virtue and gives little glory to Him Who wishes to be served by faith and *against all human hope*. But always to remain convinced that God will never forsake us, in spite of the difficulties which seem to us to be insurmountable, that His Wisdom, His Love and His Power will know how to find a way, that is true virtue, and the more a soul has passed through such trials, the higher she will attain, once she has definitely entered into God's service.[391]

4. *Charity Towards Our Neighbor*

The love of God bears with it the love of our neighbor. The first commandment is to love God with our whole heart, with our whole soul, with our whole mind and with all our strength. The second commandment is like to the first: Thou shalt love thy neighbor as thyself.[392] "Since the Incarnation," writes Dom Marmion—in those emphatic and persuasive pages which he devoted to fraternal charity[393]—"and by the Incarnation, all men are by right, if not in fact, united to Christ as the members are united to the head in the same body." Hence the life of union with God implies, as an inevitable consequence, charity towards our neighbor.

In Dom Marmion's correspondence few pages are to be found relating to fraternal charity, but these deserve to be borne in mind;

we come across more than one characterized by that fine psychology full of truth and of that luminous clearness which are one of the charms of his teaching:

The Good God is giving you the great grace of a strong and sincere desire for perfection. With this grace you ought to go far; what holds you back is that you do not give yourself up enough to God *in His members*. You would go to God *all alone* (in occupying yourself only with your individual perfection), but God presents Himself to us united to His Son, and in Him to the whole Church. If you could get out of this isolation you would make great progress.[394]

* In Holy Communion, you enter into union directly with Jesus Christ, and, through Him, with the Father and the Holy Spirit who are in Him. Again you enter with Him and through Him into union with all His members and especially with those who are perfectly united with Him in glory. This is that *Communion* for which He prayed His Father. "That they all may be one, as Thou, Father, in Me, and I in Thee; that they also may be one in Us."[395]

He beautifully develops these lofty thoughts:

The more one gives oneself to Jesus Christ, the more He gives Himself to us, and when He gives Himself to us perfectly, it is the plenitude of His life in us, holiness, and perfect union with Him. Now to give oneself to Jesus Christ is first of all to abandon oneself to Him completely, leaving to His wisdom and His love the *care* of disposing of everything for His glory and our good. The more perfect and complete this abandon is, the more Jesus Christ takes it upon Himself to rule all the details of our life.

Next, to give oneself to Jesus Christ is to give oneself to others for love of Him, or rather to give oneself to Him in the person of our neighbor. He has said, "Amen, amen, I say to you as long as you did anything to the least of those who believe in Me, you did it to Me."[396] There are so *few* people who understand this truth, that is why there are so few saints. Never forget this, my daughter: Our Lord never gives Himself except to those who give themselves to Him in the person of their neighbor. And to give you the reason for this: as God is incarnate in the Holy Humanity of Jesus Christ, He is in some manner incarnate in our neighbor, and as we can only go to God through this Sacred Humanity, therefore can we only be united to Christ by *accepting Him united to our neighbor.* Carefully meditate upon this teaching, it is very fruitful.[397]

He writes to a nun:

Ask your patron, as I do for you, to obtain for you such an ardent love for your Divine Spouse that all other love may flow from it. We may never share our love for God with any other creature; His commandment is formal: "Thou, shalt love the Lord God with thy *whole* heart." But in the same way as we love God, we may love others, *because He* loves them, and because He desires that we should love them, and in the order and degree in which He wills that we should love them.

When we love thus, our love for others takes nothing away from God, but it is, on the contrary, another form of our love for Him. To love in this way is a grace which we ought to ask of God and which we ought to try to merit by the intensity of our love for Him. Speaking of Saint Teresa an author has written: "The tender affections of her heart passing through the Heart of Jesus drew therefrom a twofold life: they became divine by their principle, they remained human in their expression; like the thrice-holy friendship of Our Lord Himself for the Apostles, His disciples, John and Lazarus, etc..."[398]

———❧———

As to the practice of charity towards our neighbor he wished it to be at once human and supernatural. Let us see how in throwing light on this doctrine he does away with scruples:

* God expects each creature to serve and love Him according to its nature. The Angels must love God *angelically,* that is without heart, sentiments, affections for they have none of these things. But He expects man to love Him *humanly,* that is with all his heart, soul, strength and mind, and *his neighbor in the same way.* We are neither spirits nor ghosts, but human beings, and we cannot go higher than perfect humanity elevated by grace.

Now Jesus is perfect humanity, perfect Deity. He loved His Mother as a child should love, not only with His head, but with His heart. He kissed her and was fondled by her and liked it. He loved all men: *a*) for their souls in view of eternity, *b*) for their *entire persons,* humanly; *c*) He loved some with a special human love. He wept when Lazarus died. Where did these tears come from? Not from His soul, but from His Heart. He did not love angelically, because He was not an angel but the Son of Man; no one was ever so human as Jesus. His Father found all His delights in Him. Amongst the creatures which God has given us to lead us to Him, and to *render our exile here possible,* are the love and affection of those who surround us. Who implanted in the mother's heart her love of her child? It was He, and how could He be displeased at our accepting this great gift! We must be on our guard not to let the devil deceive us by presenting something above human strength, and contrary to God's intentions. He has said "My yoke is light and My burden easy." It would be unbearable if we were obliged to act as *souls without bodies,* being at the same time enveloped in sense, affections and human ties despite our will. Let us be content to be as perfect as the *Man-God.* Jesus loved Mary: 1) Because He saw in her the image of His own perfection; 2) because she was His Mother.

He loved her with a child's love raised to infinite heights by the hypostatic union, but still remaining human. 3) He loved her because of all the virtues and gifts He had placed in her and so of others.

Now, my dear child, don't let your thoughts become too exalted, just act *simply* and ask Jesus to give you the gift of loving with detachment, that is, so that no human affection should *be necessary*. "One thing is necessary."[399] Use affections as you do other creatures. You will not *rest* in creatures, if you desire to use them according to God's will. See Saint Teresa keeping her niece in the convent with her, Saint Francis de Sales and Saint Chantal, Saint Augustine weeping for his mother... without a scrap of attachment.[400]

And again to the same, after she had left home for the cloister, he writes these lines so full of truth:

* Your thoughts about Jesus are too *narrow*. He isn't a bit like what you imagine. His Heart is as large as the ocean, a real human heart. He *wept* real salt tears when Lazarus died. "See how He loved him."[401] He does not expect you to be a specter or ghost. No, He wants you to be a *thorough woman* wanting love and giving it, and when you leave those you love, He wants you to *feel it deeply*. Don't be ever scrutinizing your poor little heart in fear, but look at Him. He possesses for you, His spouse, all that your poverty lacks.[402]

However as a prudent director, he is careful at need to lay stress upon certain reservations in the practice of this virtue:

Seek God's good pleasure in everything; have the intention of pleasing Him in all that you do. You have a loving heart which has need of affection, and that is why you must cleave to

God. When you are thoroughly united to Him, then He will give you a wide liberty to deal with others without any searching of heart.[403]

Writing to a monk:

I should have written to you sooner seeing that you are in trouble. But I have not found a minute. You have taken my words in an excessive, exaggerated sense. This is what I meant:

God has surrounded you with very special protection and He wants *all* your love, *all* your heart for Himself. Now the tender affection and the manifestations of this tenderness you spoke to me about, without being necessarily sin, are concessions to nature which will end by weakening your virtue. When one has reached perfect dilection, that is to say when one is *dead* to creatures, one begins a new life in which one can love without being afraid; for then the *sole* principle of this love is love of God. But you have not yet got so far. You will have to pass through many trials, "to die like the grain of wheat which falls into the ground,"[404] before being able to give your heart without fear. When Saint Teresa had passed through *long and crucifying trials,* God gave her back all her early affections. They had become stronger, tenderer, but had no more danger for her. The sign of this state is when *one has no need of these affections.* But when one is saddened and as it were helpless on being deprived of them, it is a sure sign that these affections are in part natural and imperfect and that they may enfeeble the soul and thus become an occasion of falls.

You must not rush to the opposite extreme and isolate yourself, going without the friendship your weakness needs. Only you must make use of the safeguards which prudence and the Rule lay down. I pray for you with all my heart, for I love you tenderly in Jesus Christ.[405]

Here and there are brief counsels recommending pleasant self-forgetfulness and joyous charity; is it not a Christian virtue to be full of happiness?

What Jesus desires before all things, for the moment, is that you should forget yourself so as to be at the service of others, like Jesus Who washed the feet of His disciples.[406]

I am so pleased to see that not only you are happy yourself but that you try to make others happy. You are quite right: "A sad saint is a sorry saint." When we have Jesus in our heart it is like offering Him an affront if we are sad. It is like saying, "You do not suffice for me." And Jesus is altogether ours.[407]

Be quite joyous, quite united to Jesus, quite charitable, and you will be more and more dear to Jesus, and more and more my child.[408]

He writes to a little girl a counsel most happily adapted to her age and state:

For the moment, your great duty is to be a little angel of consolation to your dear parents. You know that Jesus said, "what you do to the least of mine, you do it to Me."[409] Now this is much more true of your parents. They represent God for you and all that you do to console and help them, Jesus will take as done to Himself.[410]

And again, to the same:

Your position is not an easy one, you are only a child and the heavy and difficult task of consoling and sustaining your dear parents in their loss falls upon you. It is very difficult for a small person like you, but you are not alone. You know that when we are in a state of grace, the good Jesus dwells *always* in our heart, His great longing is to be *all* for us.

Your great duty is to console papa and mama. Be always joyful, a little angel of peace, and Jesus will love you very much. For He will take as done to Himself all that you do to console your dear parents.[411]

—⟨∞⟩—

There was one point of fraternal charity on which Dom Marmion always strongly insisted, namely, concerning the manner of judging others. We find echoes in his correspondence of his firm and grave teaching.

One of his earliest letters (November 27, 1894) contained these earnest counsels:

Watch over yourself especially as regards charity, and be sure that every time you are hard on your neighbor in thoughts or words, your heart is not inspired by the Sacred Heart of Jesus who is an ocean of compassion for our miseries and particularly loves those who never allow themselves to judge their neighbor harshly. Saint Catherine of Siena never allowed herself to judge her neighbor even when it concerned actions which were openly wrong, and Our Lord manifested to her how pleasing this was to Him. I know by my own experience how difficult this perfection is, but we should always try to reach what is the most perfect to give pleasure to Jesus.[412]

We again find the same doctrine nearly thirty years later (December 3, 1921):

Try as far as possible not to concern yourself with the imperfections of others as long as they do not come under your charge. It is a snare of the devil who aims at lessening your merit and grace. Christ *wills* that we should not judge our neighbor unless duty obliges us to do so. *Nolite judicare.* Judge not. "You will be judged by the Lord," He tells us "with the same rigor that you have used towards others."[413] Nothing disarms God's justice as regards us as the mercy we have for others.

On these occasions Dom Marmion particularly recommends prayer, which baffles the wiles of the devil, "the enemy who is so clever in sowing cockle."

Pray for those who seem to you to be acting badly, but do not judge them. God alone sees THE HEART, He alone can judge how far souls are responsible.[414]

A thought to which he gives this beautiful development, writing to a nun:

Often what hinders us from living in recollection is that we occupy ourselves too much with others. Do not stay to judge others, and do not think that you ought to tell the Superiors what you see that seems to you to be wrong in your Sisters, unless it is a duty with which you are charged. It is the devil who is seeking in this way to prevent you from being united to Our Lord. And the good God permits these temptations because they provide matter for an excellent purification. Say a prayer for the person on whom your judgment bears, and if the devil sees that each thought of this kind he presents to you is the occasion of a good prayer, he will give up these tactics. Turn at once to Our Lord and confide the thing to Him, saying, "My Jesus, I abandon that to You; as for me, I will attend to You alone, I want to be united to You." Evidently there are cases where we cannot approve the action, but do not let us judge the intention; that is between the soul and God. And the more experience I have the more I see there is only the eye of God to discern our intention and the value of our actions.[415]

On the other hand, he wrote very justly to a Mother Superior:

X is making progress in prayer and consequently in perfection. Thanks to the Good God, this progress is accompanied by

perfect submission to obedience and great gentleness and indulgence in her relations with others, without which her progress
in prayer might be held suspect. "By their fruits you shall know
them..."[416]

**It is indeed in prayer—Divine Office or private prayer—that we
draw upon the principle of wide and radiating charity, all made up
of forgetfulness of self, and for that very reason the bringer of
Divine grace:**

It is above all during the Divine Office that we consecrate
our whole being to God and to souls, and I am more and more
convinced that God's greatest graces are given to those who are
most generous at those moments. It is written of Jesus, "Surely
He hath borne our infirmities and carried our sorrows."[417]

When we are closely united to Him during the Divine Office
and Holy Mass, in His relations with His Father, with the
Blessed in Heaven and with faithful souls upon earth, we realize
those sublime words of His Sacred Heart, "That they all may be
one, as Thou, Father, in Me and I in Thee; that they also may be
one in Us."[418]

We become so to speak one with Him, when we take upon
us, with Him, all the sorrows, the sighings, the sufferings of
Holy Church and intercede in the name of all, full of confidence
in His Infinite merits. When we act thus habitually, we go out of
ourselves, we forget our own little sorrows and annoyances and
we think much more about God and souls. In return, God
thinks of us and fills us with His grace: "Give and it shall be
given to you: good measure and pressed down and shaken
together and running over shall they give into your bosom."[419]

My dear child, I am speaking to you in this way because the
more I see of religious, both men and women, the more I am
convinced that the great cause of their troubles is that most of

them think too much of themselves, and too little of Jesus and souls. If they could once and for all go out of themselves and consecrate their whole life to Jesus and souls, their hearts would become wide as the ocean; they themselves would fly upon the path of perfection: "I have run the way of Thy commandments when Thou didst enlarge my heart."[420]

CHAPTER V

AT THE SUMMIT OF UNION:
THE LIFE OF PRAYER

We need not repeat the substance of Dom Marmion's valuable conferences on prayer in *Christ, the Life of the Soul* and *Christ, the Ideal of the Monk*.[421] It is enough to recall that according to his definition, contemplation is the perfect "expression of our intimate life as children of God," a higher mode of operation of the theological virtues under the influence of the gifts of the Holy Spirit. This is why he insisted so much upon the practice of the virtue of faith, and the most confident and generous fidelity to the inspirations of the Spirit of Love.

The greater number[422] of Dom Marmion's spiritual letters—at least those that have reached us so far—are addressed not to beginners but to persons in religion who by profession, give themselves to prayer. Nevertheless, everyone may find inspiration in these counsels full of prudence and wisdom as also of confidence, which this master of asceticism so widely distributed.

Contemplation appeared to Dom Marmion so high and great a thing that he preferred it, as do the saints, to any activity:

* No amount of exterior work is as pleasing to God, as useful to the Church and souls as that loving contemplation, in which the soul allows God to act as He pleases in her. It is for that He has created her. "Mary has chosen the better part which shall

132

not be taken away from her." ...Our activity is pleasing to God just in so far as it is the "trop plein"† of our union with Him.[423]

Elsewhere he magnificently lays down the reason:

* God is calling you to interior union which is more useful to you, and more fruitful for the Church and souls than all your activity.

He goes on after having once more quoted Blosius on this subject:

You see, my child, God has created us for Himself, and we can do nothing greater than to give ourselves up to Him to carry out His wishes. To allow God to act on us in prayer is neither laziness nor inactivity. At such moments, deep down in the imperceptible depths of our soul, there is passing a *Divine* activity more precious than all our human activity. As the soul gets nearer to God, she becomes simpler and no words—no forms, can express nor formulate what she would say, but as the Church prays in her liturgy, "O God, to Whom every heart is open and to Whom every *will speaks,* and from Whom there is nothing hidden, purify our hearts by the infusion of the Holy Spirit that we may perfectly love Thee, and worthily praise Thee."[424]

This is why he so much wishes souls to give themselves to prayer:

Tomorrow we shall be keeping the feast of Blessed Ruysbroeck, one of the greatest mystics the Church has ever known. I shall have the happiness of celebrating the Mass in his honor. I will say it for myself, for you and yours, that the Holy Ghost may give us the gift of real prayer.[425]

He writes to a person in the world:

I am happy to learn that you find so much light and peace in prayer. It is a great grace, and the greatest assurance of your perseverance.[426]

---

† *Trop plein*: "overflowing abundance."

On the other hand, to one under his direction who, on account of his worldly occupations, had given up the practice of prayer, he expresses his regret:

I was sorry to learn that you have given up meditation. It is a snare of the devil, for without prayer, without contact of heart and soul with God, one never rises beyond mediocrity. It is during those moments of union of soul that God communicates His light and His life, although at times in an imperceptible manner.[427]

In his "Spiritual Works,"[428] Dom Marmion scarcely stays to go into details as to the attitude of the contemplative soul during the time of prayer. It suffices for his plan to determine the nature of the prayer, the different progressive degrees of which it admits, to establish the conditions of its unfolding and development and the desirable results it produces. In his letters we shall meet with many useful counsels.

Although, according to his way of thinking, prayer is a gift of God rather than the result of human art or skilful effort, it nonetheless requires indispensable dispositions. Among the latter he points out the habit of recollection as particularly valuable:

My dear child, I wish you to strive to live truly united to Our Lord without concerning yourself with all that happens. You are the spouse of Jesus; live with Him in the Father's bosom, that is the proper place of the spouse. But for that, great fidelity is needed. Remain recollected, not only during prayer, but throughout the day. I have more than once experienced for myself that if one is faithful to keep near to Him during the day, Our Lord reveals Himself to the soul, at one moment or another, outside the time of prayer, and then He helps us to make enormous progress. Jesus has said "If anyone loves Me, I will make My abode in him."[429] He abides in the soul that loves Him, and she lives ever with Him. At the beginning, this life of recollection requires efforts, but when the habit is taken, it becomes like a second nature. If one has joys or sorrows or difficulties one goes to Him, and then all is well.[430]

On another occasion he thus develops his thought:

This is what often hinders souls of good will from making progress in prayer, and it is your case, my child. In the morning, they make their prayer well, they receive Our Lord in Holy Communion and are very united to Him; then they leave the choir, they go to breakfast, they take up their work; they cast a little glance here, they say a word there, and they lose their recollection. And thus during the whole day, they advance and they fall back. You must accustom yourself to make a little sanctuary in your heart where you will always find Our Lord even in the midst of occupations and distractions; and then, as soon as you are alone, as soon as you have a few minutes *a fire shall flame out.*[431]

Try to gain mastery over your thoughts, because if one lets oneself go in one's imagination it is impossible to arrive at contemplation. Our head is a little like a mill which turns round all that is put into it; that is why it is very important, each time one has a few minutes in the day, not to let one's mind wander, but to direct it towards God. Without that neither recollection nor prayer is possible.

Try also not to think of your occupations outside the time you should give to them; we must take the upper hand with our occupations, and not let ourselves be absorbed by them; now this occupation that you like still dominates you too much and hence prevents you from living united with Our Lord.[432]

Another valuable disposition is the desire for a life of union with God and the spirit of peace. He writes in the first letter of direction we have of his (October 17, 1891):

* As regards your desire and attraction towards a more intimate union with God, and for a spirit of prayer, I feel from the various points you indicated that it is the Holy Spirit Who has inspired the desire, and that if you are faithful and patient, He

will in His own good time work in your soul what is for His greater glory and your perfection.

Theologians teach us that when God inspires us with an ardent desire for some gift, such as that of a spirit of prayer and when we often feel, when praying for it, great peace and confidence, it is a certain sign that He means to grant it. Your habit of frequently turning to God during work, and of purifying your intentions is an excellent aid towards the formation of this spirit of prayer, in so far as it depends on us, for never forget that a spirit of prayer is a gift of God.

You must be very careful to possess your soul in peace, as the Evil One will probably make great efforts to prevent your acquiring this spirit of prayer. As a general rule, you ought to regard as coming from the enemy any thought which agitates you, throws you into perplexity, which diminishes your confidence and narrows up your heart. The best thing in such cases is just to put the matter that perplexes you out of your mind, saying to yourself, "When I have the opportunity I shall ask the solution of this difficulty from some priest," and then go on in peace as you were before.

His concern for interior liberty is such that he does not wish a soul united with God and subject to His action to be disturbed by the remembrance of special intentions:

When a soul is submitted to God in prayer, it is a mistake to pay attention to *detailed intentions*. One glance at them at the beginning of your prayer is sufficient.[433]

*As regards your intentions in prayer, there are many souls who find that great precision and nicety in specifying various intentions in prayer interferes with the *unity* of their prayer and is a cause of anxiety and distractions. For such souls the best thing is to specify these intentions only from time to time, for example, once in the morning and then a *simple glance* of the soul is sufficient to recall them at the beginning of prayer. However, in all this, my dear Sister, follow the *attraction of the Holy Spirit* with great peace, as all anxiety is the mortal enemy of that disposition which the Holy Spirit wishes to find in that soul which He calls to a great union with Him.[434]

And again:

During prayer, you should not embarrass yourself by the remembrance of particular intentions or persons. Your union with God does all that in an *eminent* manner. Your union of love with God has as result, so to speak, to infuse blood (love, and Divine life) generously into all the members of Christ's Mystical Body. For my part, I take all the members of the Church into my heart, I adopt their intentions as my own in faith and love, and that once done, I think no more about it.[435]

The same advice that we found in his first letter of direction (1891)[436] is repeated a few weeks before his death:

Do not complicate your prayers by thinking of persons in particular; leave that to Our Lord, except in special cases. In general, for souls that Jesus calls to Himself, as is your case, He invites them by His inward inspiration when He wishes them to pray for such or such a thing or person specially.[437]

Dom Marmion has left excellent instructions on prayer in itself. He writes to a person in the world:

Do not forget that the main thing in prayer is *the contact* of the soul with God in faith through love. The soul resting, in faith, upon Jesus Christ is raised through humble love even to the bosom of God and there she sees the truth that she contemplates in God. There, love will show her the resolution that God wills her to take, and this resolution thus inspired by the light of the Holy Spirit is fruitful and stable. "The just man *gives* his *heart* to his Creator and prays in His sight."[438]

As to the character of prayer, he would have it above all affectionate, simple, true and pure. The following four extracts are addressed to persons living in the world, not in religion.

For what concerns meditation, let it be rather a prayer of the heart and of love than of the head. An excellent book for learning to meditate is Bossuet's *Élévations sur les Évangiles*.[439] Read under the eye of God until your heart is touched. Then give yourself up to love.[440]

For what concerns meditation, if your mind wanders, make it in such a way that your heart remains quietly turned towards Jesus and you will lose nothing.[441]

As for your retreat, for the present, you must do nothing with contention of mind or heart, but rather stay quietly under the eye of God whilst giving yourself to Him without reserve.[442]

With the Little Office of the Blessed Virgin, the rosary, and the Stations of the Cross, you have enough *vocal* prayers. It is good to keep oneself free in God's presence so as to be able to follow the attraction, which the Holy Spirit does not fail to give during the day, to lift up our hearts to Him.[443]

The prayer of faith appeared to him to be of special worth:

It is good sometimes, when alone with God, to stretch out our hands to Him and *look at Him in faith* showing Him the depths of our soul that His eye may penetrate into those abysses that are hidden in the recesses of the heart. Then our prayer is pure and very powerful, for the child gazes into the Father's face, seeking this face, that is to say His good pleasure: "Seek ye the Lord, seek His face EVERMORE."[444]

There is your watchword; it sums up all my direction for your soul which I want to be pure and simple like that of a child of love.

I am not a partisan of much direction above all when God has given the soul a glimpse of the beauty of simplicity.[445] God Himself is *simple,* infinitely simple, and He finds Himself in a simple soul lost in the Word. I cannot tell you what is the divine delight of the Heavenly Father, especially after Holy Communion, when He sees a soul deeply hidden in His Word, living by His life, and gazing at Him with humility and love.[446]

He writes to another nun:

For your prayer, do not be afraid of its simplicity. Go to God through Jesus Christ. He is the way and He will make you see the Divine perfections in the measure that is useful for you. Apart from the time of prayer, your Stations of the Cross, your spiritual reading, and your other devotional exercises will prevent any danger of excessive simplicity. The essential thing in the prayer of faith is to *love* and surrender oneself to God's every will.[447]

One cannot go astray in cleaving to Christ in faith:

Jesus is "the Way" and He leads where He abides, in the bosom of the Father. For those whom Our Lord leads to this end and by this way, there is no danger of illusion. Do not be curious to know anything, any mystery in *particular* but solely to know God in *pure faith* through Jesus Christ. If God wills to manifest anything in particular, remain very humble, and understand that such communications are *much less useful* to your soul than the *confused* knowledge of faith in which God communicates Himself *directly* to the soul in filling her with the *Divinity* and with *love:* "I will espouse thee to Me in faith," says the

Divine Spouse. For it is then only that one is right and true, and this Spouse is "Truth."[448]

And again he writes:

* When you feel a sweet calm take possession of your heart and soul, just remain there in silent love, and *let God act*. It is not surprising that what formerly filled you with devotion as the Passion, etc., does not excite you any longer. It will all come back again *but in another way*.[449]

The two following extracts form, in a few passages which must be given integrally, a precious abridgment of his whole doctrine:

You feel yourself to be too much carried away by outside things because you do not make your prayer well enough, and you do not make your prayer well because you are usually too abstracted.

You, who at this moment are very busy exteriorly, have need of very intense mental prayer. Unite yourself very closely to Our Lord in prayer, and thus during the day you will remain united to Him, and then your actions instead of being a cause of abstraction will become a means of union.

In prayer make acts of love, compunction and utter self-abasement; if you can succeed in making one act of perfect love during your prayer, you will come away with your soul warm and glowing, and you will be able after that to occupy yourself with exterior things without losing your interior recollection.

A prayer during which one has no thought, no feeling, but where one unites oneself to Our Lord, to the Blessed Virgin, to the Angels and Saints in their love for God, is good. As long as we are upon earth, prayer will always be a happiness because we love to unite ourselves to God; but often, too, it is a burden on account of the weight of our body and of our nature; that is why you must not be astonished if at times, although you have the desire and love for mental prayer, the time you devote to it seems long.

Our Lord says in the Gospel: "This is the work of God, that you believe in Him Whom He hath sent."[450] Faith in the Divinity of Jesus is the basis of all spiritual life; but we must have a logical faith which surrenders us entirely to Him. In prayer, my dear child, give yourself often to Jesus Christ. You must cast yourself down in your utter nothingness before Him, that will do great good to your soul. Yield up to Christ your body, your soul, your intellect, your heart; tell Him that you want Him to make of you all that He wills; abandon yourself to Him, but do not forget that to give oneself entirely to Christ is to be also given to His Mystical Body, to our neighbor.

During prayer, imagine that the Father is showing you His Son and saying to you, This is My beloved Son, in Whom I am well pleased: Listen to Him.[451] Acknowledge your utter nothingness then before this Word, unite yourself to Him in faith.

I want you thus to make your prayer in faith, staying at Christ's feet in adoration. This prayer, even if one says nothing, and if one has no consolations, gives the soul a great sense of faith and humility, the sense of the greatness of God and of confidence in Him. Unite yourself to Jesus and, with Him, yield yourself entirely to the Word. Try to spend your half hour of adoration in this way. You can also commune with Our Lord on some text of Scripture. When the imagination gives no help it is a sign that we must above all occupy ourselves in making acts of love. You can moreover be at peace; the fact that you love prayer proves that you make it better than you think.[452]

We are able by our efforts aided by grace, to reach a certain degree of perfection, but beyond that it is God alone Who can give us to attain to higher union. This work in the soul is something so delicate, so exquisite, that it is only God Who can effect it. That is why, my dear child, what I recommend you above all things, what will be the most useful for you, is prayer; for apart from the Sacraments, it is above all in prayer that God works within us.

Try then to live very united to Our Lord and to set apart every day a time where alone with God, you will find this contact, this embrace of the Spouse of your soul. It is in prayer, when we are alone with God, that He teaches us that all that is not Himself is nothing; then we do not concern ourselves any longer with our difficulties, our annoyances, we do not trouble about whether others are for us or against us; all those things are nothing whatever.

In the course of prayer God will operate Himself in your soul, but He will do so according to the measure you are generous and faithful, above all at Divine Office, then in obedience, at work, etc.

In prayer, if you feel a longing for God, a great thirst for Him, do not fear that this longing will turn you away from prayer, it is itself a prayer. Prayer sometimes takes place in a region where we cannot even perceive it.[453]

⸺ ⸙ ⸺

Dom Marmion takes particular care to teach those whom God calls to contemplation the respect and reverence they owe to the action of the Holy Ghost; he tells them too that the dark and wearisome hours of temptation ought to find them faithful. Christ Who dwells in them will be their strength:

   * When you feel invited to remain in silence at Our Lord's feet like Magdalen just *looking at Him* with *your heart*, without saying anything, don't cast about for any thoughts or reasonings, but just remain in loving adoration. Follow the whisperings

of the Holy Ghost. If He invites you to beg, beg; if to be silent, remain silent; if to show your misery to God, just do so. Let Him play on the fibers of your heart like a harpist, and draw forth the melody He wishes for the Divine Spouse.[454]

Souls like yours, called to interior prayer, are often greatly tempted in all ways, by the senses; to blasphemy, pride, etc. Don't be afraid. You can't do anything more glorious to God, or more useful for souls than to give yourself to Him...

The Word is ever in your heart, "If anyone love Me, My Father will love him, and *We* will come and take up *Our abode in* him." Yet after Holy Communion, and when near the Tabernacle, the Sacred Humanity of Jesus Christ (which is the link between us and the Word) brings us nearer to Him, and more efficaciously.[455]

In this infused prayer the soul is wholly yielded up to God and she is utterly immersed in the Divine Will. Nothing is more glorious for God nor more useful to souls:

* Your passive giving up of yourself to God's action is the *most pleasing* thing you can do for Him, and most useful for the Church. In such prayer there is often little *explicit* light or feeling, but the soul is really filled with light, and the heart with love. It is not selfish, as God created you *for Himself*, and you can do nothing greater than give yourself up to His will. The more one approaches God, the simpler his prayer becomes, till it ends in one long *sigh* after God: "God heareth the *desire* of the poor." Saint Francis of Assisi passed a whole night in one prayer, "My God and my all," and Saint Jane Chantal tells Saint Francis de Sales that for years her only prayer at all times, at Communion, Mass, Meditation was *de s'enfoncer de plus en plus dans la volonté divine*, to bury herself deeper in the Divine Will. Don't trouble the unity of your prayer by thinking of *distinct*

and *special* intentions. God knows them all, and it suffices to
remember them from time to time. While given up to God's
action in prayer, you are doing more for God's glory and souls,
than all human activity could do. God has no need of our activity. If He wants it, He will point it out to us.[456]

**To another contemplative he gives counsels which reveal the
prudent and enlightened director:**

* 1. The Holy Spirit is inviting you to passive prayer and you
must not "extinguish the Spirit" by misplaced activity. Nothing
is more glorious to God nor more advantageous for us than to
give God a free hand in our souls once He indicates His desire
to have it. Blosius says that a soul which abandons herself to
God's action without reserve allowing Him to operate as He
wishes in her, does more for His glory and for souls in an hour
than others in years.

2. Once you feel the attraction to remain in the silence of
adoration in God's presence, you must give yourself entirely to
the Holy Spirit and remain there in *pure faith.* "I will espouse
thee to Me in faith."[457] If God gives you no feeling, no sentiment, no distinct thought, just be there before Him in silent
love. During such moments He operates insensibly on the soul
and does more for her perfection than she could in a lifetime by
her own thoughts, etc.

3. If at any moment you feel attracted to petition or other acts,
follow this attraction. It is not necessary to pronounce words, or
to form *distinct* thoughts. Just present yourself and your petition
in silent prayer before God's face. He sees all that your heart is
saying, "The Lord has graciously heard the NEED of the poor."

4. The distractions are only on the surface of your soul. They
are a cross, but you must learn to despise them. Your prayer
goes on in the hidden depths of your soul, which is, as it were,

lying on God's bosom, His essence, and drinking in vast draughts of love and light.

5. If God ever speaks interior words, be sure to submit them to your director before acting on them.[458]

———∞∞∞———

It remains to point out what Dom Marmion thought on the subject of the divine call to contemplation. We have said that he saw in it the crowning point of the whole spiritual life; "the normal outcome, under the Holy Spirit's action, of the affections resulting from our divine adoption." It should be, according to him, accessible to every baptized person who is generous and of goodwill. Moreover, Christ invites all His disciples to tend to perfection that they may be worthy children of the Heavenly Father. Now perfection—in its fullness—is practically possible only if one lives by prayer. For Dom Marmion, contemplation is an infinitely precious gift, itself the fount of ineffable graces;[459] it is to this life of union that many religious are notably called.[460]

Furthermore this state of union is "exceedingly to be desired" for it is "transforming" and, as Dom Marmion explains:

far from producing pride, it gives birth in the soul to the deepest sense of its nothingness, for it is impossible for the creature to comprehend God's greatness without realizing at the same time its own littleness.[461]

Where there might be presumption and temerity would be in thinking to attain, by our own efforts, either to that plenitude of union which depends solely on the free and supreme Will of God, or in desiring those accidental phenomena which sometimes accompany contemplation.

But if it concerns what is the very substance of contemplation, that is to say the most pure, simple and perfect knowledge which God gives us therein of Himself and His perfections, and the intense love the soul derives from this knowledge, then aspire with all your strength to possess a high degree of prayer and to enjoy perfect contemplation. For God is the principal Author of our sanctity; He acts powerfully in these communications, and not to aspire to them would be not to desire to love God with our whole heart, our whole soul, our whole mind and our whole strength.

He concludes with these counsels full of wisdom:

It is clear, however, that we ought to subject this desire to the will of God. He alone knows what is best for our souls; and whilst sparing neither our efforts to remain generously and humbly faithful to present grace, nor our ardent aspirations towards higher perfection, it is extremely important to keep always in peace, assured as we are of God's goodness and wisdom in regard to each one of us.

In practice, he himself, careful to excess not to forestall the particular attraction of the Holy Spirit, was very reserved. His primary object was to establish the soul in entire self-abnegation, to ground her little by little, by means of constant fidelity, in solid virtue and to excite in her a true and generous seeking after God alone—until the call from on high should be manifested. But as soon as it was manifested, he resolutely encouraged the soul in the way that was meant for her. And he saw, with a joy equal to the respect which he had shown hitherto in regard to God's sovereign liberty, the divine glory still more than the good of the soul.

Two pages will suffice to reveal his thoughts on this subject. He expresses his joy in discovering in the soul the attraction of the Spirit:

I am happy to attest that you are so often invited by the interior inspiration of the One Who desires to possess you entirely as His spouse, to give yourself unreservedly to His love.[462]

At need, he reassures the soul; he shows her that she counts for nothing, moreover, in the matter of the Divine condescension; it is only upon misery that mercy is exercised:

* I am perfectly *certain* that despite your unworthiness and littleness, that God means and wishes to unite you *very closely* to Him. He is Master of His gifts which He bestows *freely* on whom He wishes. I wish you to give yourself up without fear to the leading of the Holy Spirit. If He unites you *even very closely* with God, don't resist, and don't be afraid. Your misery and unworthiness, which God has had the goodness to reveal to you, will protect you against illusion, and will but become more and more manifest to the eyes of your soul.

God's glory, as derived from us, consists principally in the infinite condescensions of His mercy. The more miserable and unworthy we are—provided we have a good will and seek Him sincerely—the more is His mercy exalted in stooping down to our misery. "There is more joy in heaven before God's angels for one sinner who doeth penance, than for the ninety-nine who need not penance."

There is more glory given to God when He condescends to stoop down to a poor, mean, selfish, ordinary creature, than when He communicates Himself to one of those grand, noble, superior natures which, to our eyes, seem to claim His notice. Saint Paul understood this so well. "He hath chosen the weak and despicable things of this world to confound the strong, etc., *ut non glorietur in conspectu ejus omnis caro,* that man should not glory in His sight." The triumph of the Passion, and of the merits of Jesus Christ, is attained when they lift up a poor weak, miserable creature and unite it with the Divinity. Therefore, my dear child, fear not to go whither God is certainly calling you.

He ends with those words of Blosius which occur so frequently under his pen, and adds:

And this is certain.[463]

The same thought, firm and persuasive, appears in the following lines. With a gesture of authority—where however his habitual discretion is again revealed—he delivers the soul from her apprehensions and lays the way open to absolute confidence:

* As regards yourself, there is no presumption in following the "attrait"[†] of which you speak. On the contrary it would *displease God* were you to hold back through vain fear. These strong desires are "dans l'ordre de la foi,"[‡] although very supernatural. Therefore as far as I have any jurisdiction over you—and I understand that you have given me full powers—*I wish* you to yield without fear to those invitations of grace and to continue your prayer which disposes you for such union. "A soul that gives herself up completely to God's leading, allowing Him to operate in her just as He pleases, *gives more glory to God* and does more for souls in one hour than others in long years" (Louis de Blois).

God often acts thus with very imperfect ungrateful souls, *because He likes...*

You are a *pessimistic impressionist,* but you have an inordinate fear of *good* impressions.

Believe me, your discouraging impressions are false, the others generally true.[464]

———∞———

To the practice of prayer, Dom Columba Marmion wished that of spiritual reading to be joined. What he suggests first of all is the reading of the Bible. In beautiful pages full of tender devotion he has admirably shown that no source of contemplation is purer nor more fruitful than the Holy Scriptures.[465]

What indeed is contemplation if not the movement of the soul which, touched and illumined by light from on high, penetrates

---

[†] *Attrait*: "attraction."

[‡] *Dans l'ordre de la foi*: "in accord with faith."

into the mystery of God in order to live by it? Now it is by the Word that God reveals Himself, and it is in the Gospel first of all that we find the utterances of the Incarnate Word. There we see Jesus revealing the ineffable in human words, translating the invisible in gestures comprehensible to our feeble minds, we have only to open our eyes, only to incline our heart to know and enjoy these lights.

Don't forget your reading of Holy Scripture. If during this reading you feel invited to speak to God, stop *a little*, and speak to God. I hope too that you read a life of some saint.[466]

I want you to read *attentively, simply, piously*, the New Testament, written for us by the Holy Spirit. It is there you will find the knowledge of Jesus Christ, His spirit, the spirit of prayer and everything.[467]

To help you in prayer, read chapter 15, 16 and 17 of Saint John's Gospel.[468]

How could he do otherwise than add to the Gospels the "Divine Epistles" which he himself read so assiduously?

* Try to assimilate Saint Paul's magnificent theology... I should advise you to read the beautiful little commentary on Saint Paul's epistles by Bernardin a Piconio.[469]

As to the Liturgy, as a worthy son of Saint Benedict, he justly regarded it as a most pure and fruitful fount of prayer. Beyond the convincing pages he has consecrated to this subject in his spiritual works we have a remarkable page of his taken from his letters.[470] Although it has already been published in full[471] we will here reproduce a few lines from it, as they enter so appositely into our subject:

The Liturgy, under the inspiration of the Holy Spirit, draws from the Scriptures, from tradition, and from the symbolism of the Church, a pure doctrine perfectly adapted to the spiritual understanding of the faithful...

The wording and form of the Liturgy, for example the Masses *de tempore,* are masterpieces of *doctrinal* composition. There the New Testament is explained by the Old. *The right attitude* of the soul towards God is indicated in the Collects. Little by little, the soul is imbued with them, and finds its prayer already prepared by our Mother the Church, as Jacob found the feast prepared by his mother for his father Isaac.

The great difficulty which so many persons experience in prayer comes in great part from the divorce established between individual prayer and the prayer of the Church; shut up alone in themselves, they attempt by reasoning to find out the meaning of the Scripture and no longer go to Our Lord through the Church.

As for ascetical and mystical writers he is very wide in his choice; here, as in all that deals with the spiritual life, he considers the needs of the soul, and again gives proof of that discretion which is one of his chief characteristics.

Among the authors whose works he recommends, figures Saint Francis de Sales, notably with his *Treatise on the Love of God:*

I am very glad that you take Saint Francis de Sales as an authority on meditation. It is *just* his spirit that I want for you.[472]

To contemplative souls living in the cloister he singles out Saint Teresa and Saint John of the Cross.

As we have already seen, he held the Venerable Blosius in particular estimation and often recommended his *Spiritual Doctrine,* of which he found the ascetical teaching "simple but profound."

If you can find the *Spiritual Doctrine of Blosius* it will greatly help you at present.[473]

He writes again of Blosius:

His spirit is just what I love. It is so true, so like the Sacred Heart.[474]

To timorous souls he recommends *Comfort for the Fainthearted* and the works of Saint Gertrude. "Her spirit"—he writes to a contemplative whose excessive fear held her back in distrust—"is just the antidote for your spiritual ills."[475] If there are any pages calculated to arouse confidence they are assuredly those where the great nun recounts as Herald of Divine Love, the infinite tenderness of the Heart of the Word Incarnate.

More than once, Dom Marmion recommends Bossuet's *Méditations sur l'Évangile* and his *Élévations sur les Mystères*. As to his contemporaries, he specially mentions Father Faber (*All for Jesus*), Monsignor Gay, Bishop Ullathorne and Bishop Hedley. He advises those in trouble to read the *Imitation du Sacre-Coeur* by Père Arnold, S. J., "a work full of instruction for the spiritual life, and which written as it has been," he would say, "by one who passed through many trials, contains much consolation for those whom God leads by the way of the holy cross."

He likewise suggested the reading of the lives of saints, but again in this matter, he shows rare discretion. What to him is of importance before all things is that spiritual reading should become the source of prayer:

Before beginning to read, invoke the Holy Spirit, read slowly, and if Our Lord inspires you with some good thought, or some affection, stop a little and speak to Him like a little child.[476]

Writing to a Carmelite nun, he offered this valuable advice:

A soul that has reached the point that yours has ought not to ape and slavishly imitate another: that would destroy the liberty of spirit and *the liberty of God's action within it*. The soul is too supple to enter into any frame whatsoever. If, then, when reading the life of a saint, you find something that you admire, but that *does not lead you into the* PEACE *of the Holy Spirit*, it would be mistaken to strive to imitate it. If the Holy Spirit wants this imitation, he will operate it in you in great peace.[477]

Thus does he watch over the interior development of the soul according to the recognized attraction of the Holy Spirit. Let us give also this interesting extract, of which the end is imbued with humility:

I know *The Secret of Mary* by Blessed Grignon de Montfort. For *certain souls*, drawn to it by grace, this devotion is doubtless fruitful and sanctifying. But for that it needs to be attracted to it by the grace of the Holy Spirit. As for myself, I have tried it, but it rather had the effect of giving me distractions. Father Faber says of himself, that in the beginning, he felt a strong repulsion for this devotion, but that, afterwards, he obtained the grace to practice it with great consolation and benefit for his soul. In practice, I do not use it for myself, I go to God through Jesus, and Mary helps me to know her Son and to go to Him. As for others who have an attraction for it, I encourage them, for this devotion was propagated by a Saint, and it seems to us exaggerated perhaps because we are not yet at the diapason of holiness. Try to arrive at a great humility by the spirit of adoration and reverence towards God, and all the rest will be added unto you.[478]

Mère Marie de Saint Pierre (Garnier), Foundress and Superior General of the Congregation of the Adorers of the Sacred Heart of Montmartre, died at Tyburn Convent (London), on June 17, 1924. A truly privileged soul of lofty virtue, she was called by God to very intimate union with Him. She will appear later on, without any doubt, as a saint of a high order. Dom Marmion first knew her in 1908, and since that time remained in continual relation with her until his death.

From his letters to Mère Marie de Saint Pierre we will select, as a conclusion to this chapter, several pages which will give an idea of what a holy intercourse it was that united these two souls, and of the wise and prudent counsels that the director gave to the one who confided herself to him. It is to be observed that Dom Marmion guided souls favored with extraordinary gifts *as if* they did not move in a special sphere. That was great wisdom. Without denying the particular character of the gifts accorded to them, the norms that he gives to these souls for their prayer are the norms of *faith,* of humility, of confidence and of self-abandonment, useful and indispensable to every soul of prayer.[479]

I have read in presence of God and with great attention what you tell me of your dispositions and the graces God gives you. I have *no* doubt as to the divine origin of these graces and of your prayer which bear the seal and all the marks of the divine action. What you tell me of the indwelling of Jesus and of His union with you in your prayer pleases me greatly and completely reassures me. That is also my way. For me, Jesus is *all*... I have great confidence that one day I shall be able to say in all truth, "I live, now not I; but Christ liveth in me." Then according to His promise, He will reveal to me the secrets of His Divinity. "If anyone love Me, I *will manifest* Myself to him."[480] This manifestation is the very high, very fruitful, very sure grace that Our Lord is granting you now, and if you are faithful, this grace will go to the point where you will become the privileged spouse of Jesus Christ. This grace is most precious not only for you, but also for the Church, for Jesus can refuse nothing to one whom He admits to His ineffable nuptials.

And yet you are very imperfect. That is because Jesus Christ very often chooses what is poor and *little* and miserable as the object of His bounty, "that no flesh should glory in His sight," but that we may acknowledge that all comes from Him. The very real imperfections which you confess to me do not make me doubt the reality of the grace you receive. God is the supreme Master, and He leaves you these weaknesses in order that you may *see* that these great graces do not come from you, and are not granted to you on account of your virtues, but on account of

your misery. You are a *member* of Jesus Christ, and the Father
truly gives to His Son what He gives to His weak and miserable
member. Do not be astonished, do not be discouraged when
you fall into a fault, but draw from the Heart of your Spouse—
for all His riches are yours—the grace and virtue that are wanting to you.[481]

**The guide is pleased to reassure the soul that sees her baseness and
littleness in the divine light:**

The numerous defects that you mention prove indeed that
Our Lord has cast His glance upon a very poor creature in order to heap His graces upon her, but they are not incompatible
with these graces: *Respexit* HUMILITATEM *ancillae suae*, "He hath
regarded the LITTLENESS of His handmaid."

All that God does for us is the result of His *mercy*: "All the
ways of the Lord are mercy and truth."[482] It is our *avowed* miseries that draw down His compassion. We are the members of His
beloved Son, and all our miseries are His. Then, my daughter,
fear nothing but give yourself without reserve to the Divine
action. Be, above all, on your guard against all *deliberate* movements of vanity or self-esteem, for then you leave this attitude
which attracts the gaze of God upon your soul.[483]

**It is in Christ that the soul must find the whole secret of union
with God; He is the infallible Way which leads to the Father, the
beloved Son Who draws down upon the soul the Divine
complaisance of which He is Himself the object:**

In all that you tell me about your soul, I see all the marks of
the Divine action. In spite of your infidelities, Our Lord continues to guide you Himself, and you can yield yourself without
fear to His Wisdom and Love. The Incarnate Word did all
things for His Father, and He says, *Mea omnid tua sunt*, "All My
things are Thine, O Father." That is why if you lay yourself

down *entirely* at His feet, He will take you with Him "into the bosom of the Father." "Father, I will that where I am, they also whom Thou hast given Me may be with Me." Now Jesus is always in the bosom of the Father. For that, my daughter, it needs great and continual abnegation, in order that Jesus may become the only mainspring of all your movements: "And I live, now not I: but Christ liveth in me."[484] Here we have the perfect union of the Bridegroom with the bride, a union to which He destines you if you are faithful. Then one becomes the object of a love of predilection on the part of the Father from Whom cometh down every good and perfect gift.[485]

It is above all by leaning upon Christ that the soul may hope for those interior "ascensions" of which the term is God Himself; but the suggestion is discreet, for the director knows how to respect the Holy Spirit's action:

Unless grace draws you otherwise, I recommend you to *begin* your prayer at the feet of the Sacred Humanity of Jesus Christ. He will bring you Himself, through this veil, into the Sanctuary of His Divinity. The glory of the Eternal Father is the glorification of His Son Jesus. The more we lean upon Him, the more we shall enter into the plans of the Eternal Father.[486]

In prayer he would have her fully disengaged from the solicitudes that weigh upon her; faithful to the action of the Spirit she is to abandon herself to the love of the Heavenly Father:

During prayer, yield yourself *without any fear* to the movements of the Holy Spirit; lay aside at that moment all care of temporal things, Our Lord wills it to be thus: "I BESEECH you, O daughters of Jerusalem... that you stir not up, nor make the beloved to awake, till she please."[487] These moments of abandonment to the Divine action give God such great glory and such great contentment that He wills nothing shall interrupt them. The more faithful you are to give yourself up to Him without any preoccupation as to temporal things, the more He will take them upon Himself. He has *promised* to do so. "Seek ye therefore first the kingdom of God, and His justice, and all these things shall be added unto you."[488]

The same respect for the inward grace which solicits the soul appears in the following lines:

For what regards your line of conduct in prayer, this is what I wish. When God invites you, and you perceive that it is fitting to implore the Divine mercy for your needs, you must follow this attraction, for Jesus has taught us to ask for our daily bread. But at the moments of divine union, be *entirely* at the disposal of the Spouse. Indeed, the praise, the repose of contemplation are so pleasing to God that they take the place of every other kind of prayer, and while you thus seek the Kingdom of God in you for His glory, He will look after all the rest... "and all these things shall be added unto you."[489]

Mère Marie de Saint Pierre, as we have said, was favored with extraordinary graces; her deep humility submitted them to the judgment of her guide. We will only quote two passages from the replies of the latter which will show us something of the gifts of God in this privileged soul and of the wise prudence of the one to whom she confided herself.

The operations of the Holy Trinity in your soul, where it appears to you there is an action as it were threefold in its source but one in itself, are quite in conformity with the Church's teaching, and there is nothing to fear. This sense of stupor, of holy awe on contact with the *incomprehensible* God is an excellent sign of the spirit that guides you. Therefore, my daughter, do not fear, but throw yourself with your eyes shut into God's bosom. These *intellectual* visions of the Divine perfections are very sure, and occur in a region of the soul where the spirit of falsehood cannot enter.

It is not the same with other phenomena such as *perceptible* words, or *imaginative* visions (that is to say that take a perceptible form), or revelations. Such things *can* come from God, Who is truly the supreme Master of our souls, and can there operate what He wills, but the lying spirit can slip in; there is need of great circumspection where such things are concerned. I tell you this in case they should happen to you, for then it would be necessary to communicate them to me, and not to act on them without the authorization of obedience. Not that I found in the description of your state anything whatsoever to cause me disquiet; on the contrary; I have found the seal of God on everything, but I speak to you of this in case this kind of phenomena should present itself.[490]

A little later he gives expression to the same firm and reassuring manner of speech:

I thank God and bless Him for the great graces He has given to your littleness, for all this bears the seal of the Divine action. The eagle is the *symbol* of the Divine action. Thus Saint John is the eagle because, leaving for the moment the Sacred Humanity of Jesus, he mounts up as far as the Word in the Bosom of the Father.[491] This action is rapid and all-powerful, especially in these "raptures" of which you speak, and it transforms the soul in a few instants. Yield yourself without fear to the Divine action. It is your *acknowledged* misery and littleness that attracts the regard of Him Who drew this universe and the heavens out of *nothing*. He loves, says Saint Paul, to make the poor and contemptible the object of His gifts that none should glory save in Him.[492]

CHAPTER VI

THE CALL TO UNION WITH GOD
IN THE RELIGIOUS LIFE

To that Divine Union of which the grace of baptism contains, in germ, the whole substance, Christ calls every soul. It is to all that the Savior gives the supreme precept, "Thou shall love the Lord thy God with thy whole heart, and with thy whole soul, and with all thy strength, and with all thy mind."

This precept obliges all men, whatever be the providential condition of each one; union with God, whereof love is the measure, can be attained in every state of life. The lives of the Saints prove this abundantly.

In the preceding pages we have seen how Dom Marmion speaks of union with God to very different people—children, young girls, persons living in the world, in the bonds of marriage, etc.

Nevertheless there is one state which, by its special constitution, by the more abundant and effectual help it supplies, justly merits to be called the state of perfection—it is the religious state. Those who enter this state are placed, by their vows, in particularly favorable conditions for removing the obstacles opposed to their union with God and for bringing about this union to its full extent.

More than one of Dom Marmion's letters refer to the call to union with God in the religious state. On occasion he uses his customary discretion to discern the Divine Will and his spirit of firmness to ensure this Will being followed when once it is manifested.

—⊷⊶—

The soul's attitude while waiting for God's will to be declared should be composed of humble submission and inward peace:

We will take these passages from a series of letters to a young girl:

I pray for you with all my heart and I ask Our Heavenly Father to guide you according to His holy will. I will pray especially during your retreat that God may make you to know His Holy will, for, my child, all our happiness, here and hereafter, consists in doing this adorable will.

If I may give you a piece of advice I will tell you not to worry. God will make you know His will and His designs *in His good time,* So then if you do not see very clearly during your retreat, don't torment yourself. Say to God "I want to be Thine entirely, but in Thy way."[493]

No, my child, you are not a saint. Your virtue is still very weak, but Our Lord is calling you to perfection. He wants your heart. But you must have a great reverence for the will of God Who is the *supreme* Master and Who alone has the right to call you where He wishes you to be. For the moment, God does not manifest His will clearly. Therefore let us wait in peace. I think that He does not manifest His will because the time has not yet arrived. He wants you to stay a certain time with your dear parents. There is no danger to be feared in such surroundings. While waiting to know God's will, do all for His love.[494]

And again:

God is not asking you at present to come to a decision, and if He calls you to the religious life, He will give you at the same time the attraction and the desire. The devil is trying to destroy your interior life by making you believe that, if you are fervent and faithful, you will feel yourself called. Now, my dear child, *if* God is really calling you, you would be as senseless as a stone in failing to respond to His call, for your life would be a failure. If He is not calling you, all your fervor and fidelity will never result in a vocation. I am not sure that you are called and up to the present I have no idea that you will be.[495]

He concludes with firmness:

Here then are two counselors who speak to you. I who love you very sincerely for Jesus, in whose name I am speaking; and the devil who is trying to deceive you as he deceived Eve, for he hates you.[496]

Another time, summing up his teaching on this subject, he writes these two lines full of confidence:

God *loves you,* and He is preparing your future according to His love; give yourself up to Him without fear and without care.[497]

⸺⸺

As soon as God's will has been ascertained the greatest generosity must be exerted in following its indications despite all the obstacles that come in the way. Dom Marmion to a young man:

Every good vocation has to be tested. But if you are faithful, Our Lord will sustain you by His grace, and you will enter the monastery with all the more joy in that you have endured trials for Our Lord. I bless you from the bottom of my heart and I will pray that you may be courageous and faithful.[498]

And again a few months later:

The more a vocation is opposed the stronger are the roots it pushes down and the more it is valued in the end.

Keep *all* your heart for Jesus Christ. If you have the courage to content yourself with His love, He will give you later on the grace of loving without attaching yourself to creatures. Work *hard*, and for Him.[499]

Very often, the most diverse objections rise up in crowds. In the supernatural light of faith, Dom Marmion knows how to dissipate them and thus to overthrow all the devices of the prince of darkness. Several letters to a young girl[500] contain on this subject instructions all steeped in the spirit of the Gospel; it will be seen how he points out and refutes the whole series of objections, sometimes quite contradictory ones, which in these circumstances preoccupy the mind:

I say to you on the part of God, *Veni filia:* "come my daughter"; against all the reasonings of the world and the flesh, set this thought, *"Jesus calls me* to be his spouse." In the world she who loves leaves all—father, mother, friends, everyone, to follow *a man*; and Jesus, the *Son of God* Who has given even the last drop of His blood for you and has heaped special blessings and graces upon you, does He not deserve that you should leave *all* when He honors you with the invitation to unite yourself more intimately with Him? I am not at all astonished at the opposition and difficulties that you are meeting at this moment. I was expecting them. God's best graces must be purchased by suffering, and it is upon the cross that Jesus Christ founds His great works. His holy Mother, whom He loved more than all other creatures, was not exempt from this law; He did not require her to renounce the affection of a sister or a mother, but to stand by the cross of Calvary, beholding her Son, her God, die in horrible torments.

I consider these difficulties, this opposition as a proof that Our Lord wants you to be entirely His, and that He means to purify you by these bitter trials so that your sacrifice be wholly pure and exempt from all self-love.

Those who are in the world and especially our parents, however good and fervent they be, have not always the light to know God's will in these matters. For the eye of their soul is obscured by human motives, and their judgment is biased by the ties of blood, without their perceiving it. The motives they allege are reasons of human prudence, and having weighed them in God's presence I am convinced that you ought not to listen to them.

And first of all, the good that you do in the world. God has no need of our works, and they only please Him in so far as they are done according to His will. And if we persist in doing what in itself is good, but after having been called by God to other things, God will no longer accept what we do; our works in this case rather displease Him, as being something that we prefer to His will. Look at Saul. Preferring human reasonings to the light of faith, he spared the best of the flocks to *offer in sacrifice* to God. What deed could be holier than offering sacrifice to God? And yet Holy Scripture tells us that for this infidelity, God rejected Saul.[501] Now I say to you Jesus Christ does not want *your deeds,* He wishes to have you yourself, and He will not accept any other gift. Turn to God and leave to Him the care of providing for the continuation of your good works.

Although I speak so severely, I have the greatest compassion for you in my heart and I recommend you much to God in my prayers, but I fear lest you should not respond to grace. Our Lord said "He that loveth father or mother more than Me, is not worthy of Me." Saint Jane Chantal had much stronger family reasons than yours for remaining in the world, above all as it was not a question of entering an already existing community, but of founding an order herself. She felt, like you, all the bitterness of separation from her own kin; on every side she heard her project treated as extravagant and imprudent, she saw the poor begging her on their knees to stay in the world and continue her good works for them, but she would rather have died than fail in fidelity to Him Who called her.

Courage! Jesus is calling you to be His spouse. Hold on to that. Believe me, you will do as much good (and a thousand times more) to your family in giving yourself to God than in remaining in the world. For God is the source of all true good, and He knows how to do Himself all that He would have done through you. Arm yourself then with thoughts of faith. Show no hesitation. Accept with *perfect resignation* these very painful sufferings that Jesus is now sending you, they are a proof of His love for you. Be quite determined, and you will see that your difficulties will diminish. For it is when your parents see you hesitating and undecided that they will do all they possibly can to shake your resolution. Almost all those whom God calls to the religious state have to pass through similar trials, without which they would not be worthy of the nuptials of the Lamb.

The only thing that makes me anxious is lest these trials should injure your health. That is why I should like to see you enter as soon as that can be suitably arranged.

I am very interested in you in Our Lord and pray much for you. Write to me as soon as you will and just as your heart inspires you.[502]

If Jesus is making you suffer at present, it is because He is treating you as He treats all those He loves and calls to more intimate union with Himself. If you had not these trials, I should have some fear for your vocation, but trial, and especially those that come from our affection for those dear to us, bear the divine seal of the holy cross.

I advise you not to say much when objections or reasonings are made against your vocation. Content yourself with saying, "After having prayed a great deal, and asked the advice from my confessor, I am convinced that God calls me and that I should be failing in correspondence to grace in refusing to follow Him." Don't enter into discussions that serve for nothing, but listen silently and commend yourself to God.[503]

I feel *great compassion* for your poor sister and your mother, but Jesus felt an infinitely greater compassion for His holy Mother and for Saint John and the *holy women* who were at the foot of the Cross, and yet He willed that they should drink the chalice to the last drop. And since God wishes to sanctify you by this sorrow, I am entirely conformed to His designs and I want you to try every day to enter further into these dispositions by meditation and union with Jesus suffering.

As I told you the other day, it is very important that, during this time, you should devote yourself, with all your heart, to your usual good works, as if you had the intention of continuing them always. All we do for God is worth the trouble of doing well.

As the devil is very discontented at your decision to enter the cloister, it is not impossible that he may raise up other exterior and interior difficulties and, to this end, transform himself into an angel of light. So then if any serious difficulty befalls you, say, "I decide nothing before having consulted God and my confessor." I will pray very much for you until I see you very comfortably settled in the nest with the other doves.[504]

The time that the holy will of God obliges you to spend in the world (before your entry into the cloister) not only is not lost, but is doing a work in your soul that is necessary for your advancement in virtue. The Good God desires to see in you complete submission, *absolute abandon* to His holy will and it is for that reason He goes against your own will even in holy things in order there may remain in you only one will, "that of doing God's holy will." Many people think they have an entire submission to God's will, but one sees by their grief and discontent—when they are hindered from making their spiritual exercises to which they are attached—how much they are wanting in holy indifference. Our Lord revealed to a certain person that what pleased Him most in Saint Gertrude was her *liberty of spirit,* that is to say her complete detachment from all things, even holy things, to cleave solely to God's will.

He gives the same counsels of generosity and peaceful waiting to a future Carmelite:

October 4, 1900.—Keep very firm in your vocation. Our Lord wants you a Carmelite and nothing else. Tell that to the devil when he suggests anything else. All these considerations as to the usefulness of your life in the world, of ingratitude towards parents, etc., are only temptations, and part of the trial which renders your sacrifice so glorious for Him Who has deigned to choose you as spouse, and so meritorious for you. Without these combats and heart-rendings, your entering Carmel would not sufficiently bear the seal of the cross.

July 25, 1912.—It is certain, *with the certainty of faith,* that what we ask in reference to our salvation and in the name of Jesus Christ will be granted to us. Now to carry out God's plans for our souls certainly refers to our salvation. Then if you continue to pray with absolute confidence in Him Whom you hope one day to call by the sweet name of Spouse, it is certain that nothing will be able to prevent you from following your vocation. It is when things appear, humanly speaking, to be lost that Our Lord likes to show His wisdom and love which overthrow all the plans of men, and when we can do nothing more, Our Lord takes upon Himself to intervene... If, despite *all*, Our Lord makes you wait a little, be sure, my child, that He has His views of Wisdom and Love.

November 13, 1901.—I am delighted to see that you are remaining closely united to Our Lord. All is in that. I am so convinced that since you abandon yourself altogether to Jesus, He is directing everything with infinite Wisdom and Love for your greatest good, that I cannot be sorry for this delay He is imposing on you. Certainly I long to see you among my dear children of Carmel to form you for my Divine Master, but I submit myself entirely to His designs for your soul. He is the Master.

* As regards your fears of selfishness, you know that God is "the Lord" and that He has the first call on us. "He who loves father or mother more than Me, is not worthy of Me." Ordinarily on entering religion, our greatest pain, is the pain we cause others. The whole question is *does* God call you, and I must say, unless you wait for a revelation, it would be hard to have greater evidence. You are not necessary to your mother, and so if Jesus calls you to "leave father and mother and sisters and brothers etc., and follow Him," He has a right to be obeyed, and your happiness, and that of these you love, may in great measure depend on your fidelity in this matter.[505]

In other circumstances—he has just hinted as much—the duty of filial piety is evident and not to be evaded; Dom Marmion wishes then it be accepted even at the price of the momentary sacrifice of higher aspirations, in view of the clearly manifested Divine will:

Our Lord is at this moment setting you an arduous task, for you must forget yourself and give up for the time being the most cherished and sacred aspirations of your heart, in order to fulfill the duty of filial piety that circumstances exact. I understand your position perfectly. Your dear parents have made a sublime sacrifice in an heroic manner. But nature is there. They must be sustained by the grace that will not fail them and also by that affection of which your heart is so capable. Yes, my dear child, they need your smile, your affection which will make up as far as possible for the one they have lost. Even though your heart bleed, they must not see it.

I cannot tell you how pleasing such a task is to the Sacred Heart. Believe me, you could not, for the moment, be doing anything more meritorious, more sanctifying, more agreeable to Him Whom you love than to testify your love, your self-forget-fulness by lavishing them upon your dear parents and those around you. The more such a way of acting is hidden, the more it is only known to Jesus—the more pleasing it is to Him.

As I promised, I will help you by praying for you every morning at the Holy Sacrifice and by my sincere and faithful devotion. Be sure that you will only be gaining (by acting in this way) and when the time comes for you to enter the cloister, you will receive *choice graces* that will make of you that holy religious I dream and for whom I pray with all my heart.[506]

Dom Marmion's charity was so large-hearted and his solicitude so alert that it extended to the near relatives of those whose vocation he directed. Two letters reveal his tact and supernatural firmness tempered with exquisite kindliness:

My dear friend, thank you very sincerely for the confidence you show me in consulting me on this important matter of your dear daughter's vocation. After having well reflected and having prayed Our Lord to make me know His holy will, I will tell you in all sincerity what I think before God.

A greater sacrifice cannot be offered to God than that of a tenderly loved child. That is why God wishing to choose Abraham as the father of the faithful asked of him the sacrifice of his beloved son Isaac, and because Abraham did not hesitate to give back to God this son that he had received from Him, the Lord blessed him and poured upon him and all his posterity the greatest heavenly blessings.

I understand, my dear friend, that this sacrifice will be no less hard for you. N... has great qualities of mind and heart, and her parents certainly have a right to expect from her, in return for the sacrifices they have made for their children, that consolation and support she would be able to give them. I even confess that, for nature, this sacrifice would appear too hard. But I remember that I am writing to a sincere Christian who would refuse nothing to his God, provided he had the certainty that it was truly His holy will.

Well! I am convinced before God that your child has a true religious vocation, that Our Lord is calling her to Carmel, and that He wants you to give her the permission even now. In ordinary cases, one would hesitate before allowing one of her age to enter Carmel. The nuns themselves assured me that they would never accept such young persons without the certainty of a vocation, and my personal opinion is that before undertaking such a life, it is necessary to be quite assured that all the importance and gravity of the act has been thoroughly understood. Now I am convinced that your daughter's character is so formed, her judgment so sure, that there is not the least indiscretion in admitting her to Carmel at once and that is the opinion of the nuns themselves and of the Father Provincial who approves of her immediate admission. I tell you then, my dear friend, I am sure that Jesus Christ expects this sacrifice from you, and I assure you that this sacrifice will be your sweetest consolation during your life and a source of great confidence at the hour of death. I remember that my dear father, after having given two of his daughters to Jesus Christ in religion, hesitated about granting permission to the last and dearest of his daughters. Finally, not able to refuse anything to Jesus Christ, he granted it in spite of himself. Now shortly afterwards, being upon the point of appearing before the Sovereign Judge, he declared that his greatest consolation at that moment was to have given to Jesus Christ what was the dearest to him in the world.

I counsel you then, dear friend, to receive Holy Communion, and then, in the intimacy of that sacramental union, to offer your child to Jesus Christ as His spouse, asking Him to receive her from your hands, and I, in His name, promise you His Divine blessing for you, and those dear to you.[507]

My dear friend, I have just received your note and I bless the Good God for having given you the light to understand the true interests of your dear child. One day, you will realize the price of your sacrifice and will rejoice during all eternity for having given to God what is *so* dear to you.

After having carefully reflected before God, I say to you on His part to offer your dear child to Him on September 24, Feast of Our Lady of Mercy. On that day I will ask Mary to receive this dear child from your hands and to do for you and for your dear family all that N... would have wished to do if she had stayed at home. Mary will be a mother for you and will render you a hundredfold what you have sacrificed out of love for her Divine Son.[508]

It may happen that after an honest attempt, the religious life is shown to be impracticable. The soul is then often left helpless, all seems to be lost, even on the side of heaven. A particularly painful state for those of high ideals who yearn for great union with God. In such circumstances Dom Marmion knew where to find words to enlighten and encourage: perfection is not to be found necessarily and exclusively in the religious state; quiet and peace of soul, like union with God, are to be found only in confident abandonment to the Divine will:

* How far you are from sounding the depths of Our Lord's heart, and of its love for you! There is no question of a want or a diminution of love. He loves you dearly, and you *are* His dearly beloved little spouse. His strong arm encircles you and His hand bears up your head, as you repose on His Heart.

The fact of living in a cloister is a mere accident and cannot effect or diminish your love, if, as in this case, it comes from His wish, from His mysterious designs on your soul. Saint Joseph Labre, who is a great Saint, canonized and venerated by the Church, had a most powerful attraction for our Benedictine life. He entered several times (3 times I think) and after doing his best, was obliged to leave. He became a *Saint*, which he most probably would not have been in the cloister, *because* it was not the way Jesus had chosen for him. A Saint's whole life may be summed up in these words of the holy Liturgy, "This man accomplished all that God commanded him."[509] That is *perfection*.

I know you *perfectly* now,—I assure you 1) that Jesus loves you dearly. 2) That He is quite satisfied with the efforts you made to carry out what you thought to be His will. 3) That you can attain just as high perfection and just as close union with Him, by performing with *great love, great patience with yourself,* and great humility, the task which His will sets you daily.

I assure you it is the demon who tries to cast darkness and distrust into your soul. There is nothing Our Lord demands so much from His lovers as "hoping against hope" just trusting in His loyalty, His fidelity, His Love; and nothing so wounds Him as any distrust or want of confidence.

After having, according to Saint Paul, given the example of Abraham's faith and confidence concerning Isaac, he continues:

You look too much at your littleness, at your miseries, at your shortcomings, and too little at Jesus. He is so great, so loving, so *faithful*—so wise—so powerful. Say often, "O Sacred Heart of Jesus, I have confidence in You," even though you don't feel it—*feelings do not matter.*

There is a little leaflet by Monsignor Goodier, S.J. Archbishop of Bombay, called "A More Excellent Way." It is published by the Sacred Heart nuns at Roehampton... It will *just* suit the state of your soul and say fifty times better than I could what I have been saying.

P. S. Neither Our Lady, nor many of the holy virgins and spouses of Jesus, Thecla, Agatha, Agnes, lived in a convent, yet they were perfect spouses of Jesus.[510]

Even when he has pronounced his vows in an Order, the religious is not secure from temptations regarding his profession. Man's inconstancy is such that the longing for change easily finds access to his mind. The temptation to pass from one Order to another, wrote Dom Marmion, is classic with novices. It is found even with professed religious. In this case, Dom Marmion was particularly solicitous to discover what was God's will. To one of his monks who expresses his desire to go over to the Carthusian Order, he replies:

I read your letter most attentively. Then I prayed with all my heart, for I have great respect for God's rights and would not for *anything in the world* substitute my ideas or wishes for the designs of His adorable Providence. I think I have set aside all that could have influenced my judgment, my great fatherly affection and *quite especially* for you, the thought of your parents, the services you could render etc. I believe I placed myself *sub oculo Dei*, under the eye of God, in a state of complete abandon to His will, having as my *sole* desire that of knowing and doing His will. Moreover, as Abbot, I have a right to expect from God an altogether special grace and light for the direction of those belonging to me. Now I have the certainty that this is not God's will, and that if you enter in that way, you will lose your monastic vocation and will end by returning to the world. It often happens (it has happened to myself and to several others) that this thought (of passing to a more austere Order) arises in the mind of those who long to consecrate themselves more closely to God's service. God takes their good will into account. But, as our Blessed Father Saint Benedict says, in speaking of this kind of monk, "they ought not to be of those who are in the *first fervor* of religious life, but of those who after long probation in the monastery have learnt by the help and support of many brethren to fight against the devil."[511] I have spoken with experienced Carthusians and they acknowledge that those only make good monks who have *great* fervor and *great* strength of will; others run the risk of spending their time in idle reverie and do little for God or their neighbor. Father Prior and Father Master quite share my opinion. I cannot then approve of your project to make a retreat with the Carthusians. The only result would be to make you live in an ideal, imaginary world, while you would take a dislike to the life to which God has called you. God's will for the present is without *any doubt* that you bravely take up the cross *of your duties of state performed as perfectly as possible* (studies, etc.) upon your shoulders. Apart from that is only illusion and self-seeking. I bless you with all my heart, and pray for you.[512]

We have the good fortune to possess several of Dom Marmion's letters to a young man whom he directed to Carmel.[513] On the occasion of each of the great acts which mark the principal stages of all religious life, Dom Columba wrote to his spiritual son letters containing the loftiest teaching. It is needless to emphasize their luminous clearness. Despite a few incidental repetitions, none would wish us to refrain from giving these letters in full.

December 27, 1903.—Your kind letter greatly consoled me and I thank Our Lord from the bottom of my heart for having used me to make known to you His holy will and to encourage you in the difficulties that every true vocation must encounter. I feel more and more how much I am a useless servant in the hands of Our Lord Who yet is so good as to employ me in His service, and your promise to remember me at the holy altar is a *very great consolation* to me. For my part, I will never forget you until we be united forever in that beautiful paradise of the Heavenly Father.

Enter religion *without project, without plan* save the project of belonging *entirely* to Our Lord and of being the most little, the most submissive of religious to those whom God wills to employ to represent Him (towards us). You will be a good religious in the measure of your submission and obedience. Never forget that in entering religion, and above all on the day of your profession, an implicit contract is established between God and yourself. God engages to bring you to His perfect love through those who represent Him, and He is wise enough and powerful enough to fulfill His part of the contract, whatever those who represent Him may be. On your side, you undertake one thing only—to let yourself be guided by your Superiors. Sometimes, to try your faith and your fidelity, He will allow your Superiors to ordain things that might seem contrary to your sanctification (for instance: they may refuse you permission to perform mortifications), but if you have faith, "all things work together for good."

I will pray specially during the days preceding your entry, for I know that the devil will do all he possibly can to prevent you following your vocation, or, if he does not arrive at doing so, he will try to dissipate your soul so that it will not be well disposed on entering the novitiate; now this good disposition is most important.

January 31, 1905.—At last you are in the house of the Good God and entered upon your way. Having made so many sacrifices, having left all, do not hesitate before any sacrifice as soon as you know that Our Lord asks it of you. For I am convinced that a religious is happy and becomes an instrument for God's glory according to the degree of his absolute abandon to the will from on high.

I am so happy to see that you are going to make a thorough study of the principles and spirit of your Order. Religious are distinguished not so much by their habit and the customs of their Order as by the interior spirit which is the soul of their institute. There are so many who only wear the habit of their Order, and know neither its spirit, nor history, nor ascetic teaching! They set aside the magnificent works written by their founder and their saints for the forming of subjects and they draw *all* their inner life from other sources.

The reason for our vocation is the desire that Our Lord has of being served and glorified according to the spirit of the Order to which He calls us. As for you, you have such pure, such substantial, such authorized nourishment for your soul in the writings of your Mother, Saint Teresa, of Saint John of the Cross and other writers of your Order, that it would be a crime to *form* yourself by drawing at other sources.

I end now, my dear Brother, in leaving you henceforth in the hands of your good Superiors. Be *like a child* with them. They are the oracle through which God will speak to you. I will pray to God for you and for myself and we shall thus remain united in the Sacred Heart. I advise you to shut yourself up very closely with Jesus and Mary during these months of your novitiate, for all your religious life depends on them.

November 26, 1906.—Your dear letter was a real joy to me. You tell me that Our Lord is admitting you to the happiness of being united with Him perfectly and for always. I have prayed very much for you that you may pass through the dangers and temptations that the devil so often holds out to us during the novitiate.

I will go on praying with more fervor during all this time between now and your holy profession that this act may be for you a perfect and definitive sacrifice. Profession contains in germ all religious holiness, and to arrive at the perfection of this sublime vocation, one has no need to seek beyond this *capital* grace. *A religious profession* faithfully observed leads *infallibly* to holiness. It so often happens that the demon deceives us on this point. He suggests to us that if we were employed more in such or such kind of good work, we should make great progress. Never forget, my very dear brother, what I am going to say to you. On the day of our profession a contract is concluded between us and God. We bind ourselves to let ourselves be guided by holy obedience, and God binds Himself on His side to bring us to Himself, provided that we leave ourselves *with faith* in the hands of our Superiors.

Then give yourself to God without reserve, and without desiring anything in particular. He knows what you are and what you can do, and so leave things to Him. I think you will do *much* for God if you abandon yourself humbly into His hands.

January 27, 1907.—I send you these lines to offer you my fraternal congratulations and my good wishes for your perseverance and perfection.

After more than twenty years of monastic life, I can tell you that the more one remits oneself into God's hands *for everything,* the more one lives in ABSOLUTE dependence on His good pleasure, the more He supports and blesses us in all that we do.

Our Heavenly Father is the Fountainhead, *Fons vitae,* and the primary Principle of all, *and we honor Him in leaving the initiative to Him* in all things. Religious who make plans and projects for the future, and especially those who try to bring them about by little human means, *are never at peace and do nothing that is worthwhile.*

On the blessed day of our profession we make a contract with God. On one hand, we bind ourselves to give ourselves over to Him under the guidance of obedience, and God, on the other hand, binds Himself to bring us to His *perfect love* through those Superiors whom He sets over us. "Thou hast set MEN over our heads,"[514] despite their faults, their errors. *This sacrifice of obedience is the greatest* we can make. At times obedience is sweet and easy, at times God permits that those under whose guidance He places us cause us great suffering. But if we keep *the eye of faith* fixed upon Him Who rules all things, and *without Whose permission nothing can befall us,* we shall accept all without being moved. It is a very serious thing to give oneself thus without reserve into God's hands. He is Infinite Love, but at the same time "a consuming fire."[515] Jesus, at the moment of His Incarnation, gave Himself thus without reserve into the hands of Infinite Love: "In the head of the book it is written of me: that I should do Thy will, O God... Then I said: BEHOLD I COME that I should do Thy will."[516]

And how did Infinite Love treat this Jesus:

It gave Him over to the scourges, the spittle, the thorns, the ignominies of Calvary. And if Love thus treated the green wood what will it do with us who are so fit to be burnt?

I say this to you, my dear brother, for I long so much to see you become a perfect religious who refuses nothing to this God Who has given us so much.

Keep thoroughly in the spirit of your vocation, for whatever be the good works we do outside our vocation, we shall only please the Good God in doing that which we have promised. Now in the same way as I have promised to be a Benedictine, you are going to promise to be a Carmelite, and you will be pleasing to God in the measure you carry out the ideal of your vocation. A glorious vocation which in prayer, solitude and penance draws upon the treasure of grace which it pours from its overflowing abundance upon souls. One truly united with God *by prayer and dependence on His good pleasure* does more for souls in a week than others who live apart from this union with God do in their whole life. "Paul planted, Apollo watered: BUT GOD GAVE THE INCREASE."[517]

This is, my dear brother, my ideal for you and for myself, the object of my most ardent good wishes and of my daily prayers.

CHAPTER VII

Union with God
in Superiors

Among Dom Marmion's letters, many are the pages addressed to Superiors of religious Communities or to Novice Mistresses. We will select several; they will reveal the lofty doctrine that this master of asceticism gave to souls charged to direct others in the path of perfection.[518]

Oftentimes this is a heavy charge! In the chapter on the father of the monastery—a chapter wherein the admirable counsels resulting from experience can be applied to every Superior—Saint Benedict most forcibly insists, in several places, on the formidable responsibility which weighs with good reason upon them.[519] "Let the Abbot," writes the great Legislator, "hold it for a certain truth that on the Day of Judgment he will have to give a strict account to God not only of his own soul but of those of all the brethren under his care. This wholesome fear of God's inevitable judgments will make the Abbot attentive, and in the care he must take in directing Christ's sheep, he will find the occasion of keeping himself pure and stainless in God's sight."[520]

Those who have light to grasp the full meaning of this grave responsibility are naturally alarmed. To constant spiritual solicitude are added incessant anxieties of a material order; the multifarious cross-purposes arising from extreme diversities of character, the difficulties and annoyances that daily occur, continual self-abnegation, all that which Dom Marmion called "being eaten up alive at each moment"[521] and it will be easily understood how souls, above all contemplative souls recoil from such a heavy burden:

* It is *impossible* that Our Lord should command you by the voice of obedience to undertake anything which would be detrimental to your soul. It will seem to you at times that the task imposed is above your strength but God is *bound* to give you all the light and grace necessary to fill an office in which He Himself places you.[522]

Therefore he insists on this point. To a Carmelite mistress of novices who makes the most of her inaptitude for this mission he recommends confidence:

You should remit yourself *without counting the cost* into the hands of the Heavenly Father. Nothing is so dangerous as to withdraw from His hand, even under the holiest pretexts.

And alluding to the Biblical incident where Samson, upon the Lord's command, puts the Philistines to flight with the jawbone of an ass—an application which coming from his pen to one of his especially dear daughters had nothing offensive in it—he adds:

The jawbone of an ass in God's hands is worth more than a sword of steel in any other hand. To refuse charges laid upon you by God is to be wanting in humility and confidence.[523]

When one abandons oneself into God's hands, what is most perfect as well as most sure is to accept His every will with childlike confidence. It is not forbidden to make known one's repugnances and incapacity but this once done, as my Blessed Father Saint Benedict so well says "one ought to obey for the love of God, trusting in His assistance."[524] I know very well that your charge will be a very heavy one, but God is bound to help you, and you are bound to devote yourself to it, even if that should turn to your confusion.[525]

—⁓—

Apparently more serious, surely more subtle, is the pretext drawn from the difficulty of safeguarding intimate union with God in the midst of the multifarious cares of superiorship. To a Mother Superior who, in spite of his warnings, has incessant recourse to this pretext to liberate herself from the burden laid upon her by obedience, Dom Marmion pronounces the firm and sure language of faith which frustrates the hidden ruses of the Spirit of darkness; he shows her the danger of these illusions in which she risks losing her soul:

When praying for you, I understood that the *complete and confident* submission of yourself to God's holy will is the *one* thing Our Lord asks of you. Apart from this holy will all is illusion and danger, whatever peace or consolation you think you might find by escaping from it. Holy Scripture tells us, *Sunt viae quae hominibus videntur rectae...* "There are ways that seem to men to be good, but they end in the deepest hell."[526] Our Lord is calling you to His perfect love, but He meets with much resistance on your part which hinders His operation and afflicts His Sacred Heart. This resistance comes from three causes:

1. A want of generosity; you prefer your own tranquillity and consolation to the glory of Jesus;

2. Attachment to your own judgment: instead of following eternal Wisdom manifested by the voice of your (major) Superiors, you would impose upon Our Lord your own way of looking at things.

3. The obscurity of your conscience: this obscurity proceeds from a withdrawing of grace and light which is a punishment for your want of abandonment.

Believe me, my dear daughter, I am speaking in the name of Jesus Christ. The only way for you to arrive at peace and holiness is that of entire abandonment to the Wisdom and Love of Jesus. Here is a fragment of a letter from Saint Francis de Sales to one who was in a position similar to yours. You see that your poor father does not tell you anything different. "Live all for God, my dear daughter. Do not think that Our Lord is further away from you when you are amidst the worries your charge involves upon you than He would be if you were in the midst of the delights of a tranquil life. No, my dearest daughter, *it is not tranquillity that brings Him near to our hearts,* it is the fidelity of our love; it is not our sense of His sweetness, but our consent to His holy will, which it is more desirable should be done in us than if we did our will in Him."[527]

Therefore Dom Marmion rightly concludes:

Be persuaded, my daughter, that as long as you refuse to give yourself up blindly to His holy will, you will seek for peace in vain, for, if overcome by your entreaties, your (major) Superiors grant you permission to withdraw from your charge and to live in solitude, this permission extorted from them would not be the expression of the Divine will, and even if in this state you felt heavenly delights showered upon you, I should regard all that as suspect and a mere illusion from Satan. So be a little child, and lean upon your Divine Spouse.

And these are now his practical counsels:

So that the devil may no longer succeed in turning you away from God's will, take the following resolutions:

1. Never reason within yourself on the orders of Superiors; if you have any trouble, tell *me,* freely, but in all submission.

2. Give Our Lord the glory that is due to Him: rest upon Him with confidence despite your misery and incapacity.

Nothing is more glorious for Jesus Christ than the faith of a weak, miserable person who rests in Him. *Revela Domino viam tuam et spera in Eo, et Ipse faciet.* "Reveal thy way to the Lord, and trust in Him, and He will do everything."[528]

My dear daughter, these few words are written by your poor father who, in spite of his misery, loves you sincerely in Our Lord; He prays much for your advancement in Divine love.[529]

These supernatural views which he requires of a Prioress in regard to her major Superiors, he wishes should be held likewise in the relations existing between the Prioress and Mistress of Novices of the same house. This domain is a delicate one. The director in his wisdom points out the principle of the solution which will remove difficulties and safeguard that union so necessary for the welfare of souls:

The position [of a Mistress of Novices] in regard to the Prioress is very *delicate*; only great simplicity and purity of outlook can resolve it. The Prioress has *the grace of state, the protection and direction of the Holy Spirit, because she holds the place of Jesus.* No gift of intellect, nor any virtue, nor personal illumination will have for the Community the fecundity of that grace which is hers. All the gifts of nature and grace bestowed upon you by Our Lord must be communicated with great humility and perfect generosity in order to be productive of good through your grace of state. Meditate on that.[530]

<hr/>

What does Dom Marmion ask of those who are invested with the exercise of authority? He especially asks for self-abnegation and devotedness to souls: are they not placed in command for the common good?

For you, my dear daughter, what is most necessary is to go out of yourself and to *devote* yourself to Jesus and His members. The more you leave yourself, the more Jesus will take His delights in your soul. Each time that you feel the movements of self-love in its various manifestations—sensitiveness, sadness, the desire to occupy attention, discouragement—make the sacrifice of it at once to Jesus.[531]

In this total and disinterested devotedness, Dom Marmion sees, with reason, one of the most evident proofs of love for God:

The love with which we act is the key of our life. We cannot think about that too much; one would quickly become a saint if one was very zealous to do each action with great love.[532] I was reading yesterday with much pleasure the magnificent articles of Saint Thomas on the object of devotion (II-II, q. 82). Devotion is the flower of love. "Simon, son of John, lovest thou Me more than these? Feed My sheep."[533] To give oneself to others, or rather to give oneself to Christ in the persons of His members, is the real proof of love. It is for this that God has chosen you from all eternity to be Superior, and a perfect Superior is a mother giving herself as never mother in the world gives herself to her children. It is hard, but it is great! "Christ loved the Church, and delivered Himself up for it."[534] All is in that for you: HE DELIVERED HIMSELF. It is that which will destroy in you all that remains of that little N... [name of the religious in the world] which is not yet entirely subject to the action of Christ.[535]

He writes to another Superior:

Try to sanctify souls for Jesus. At our religious profession we give ourselves to Him without reserve. Now for His sake let us give ourselves to those who are His members.[536]

As this love ought to enfold all souls, since Christ lives in each one of them, he writes:

See Jesus in *all* the souls confided to you, Jesus weak, Jesus narrowed down, but certainly there.[537]

* X... is a difficult case. She wants simplicity, and that is so hard to teach; and yet without it direction only complicates things more. Let her learn to seek God *alone* and all will come right.[538]

He writes again:

Every Superior who seeks God simply and sincerely has the right to a special grace *of state* to enlighten her. Your estimate concerning Sister N... is true. Take it into account in order to prevent abuses, but not to prevent your love... Leave all to Jesus. As long as we keep our eyes only fixed upon Him to know and carry out His will, His designs, He will take care of everything.[539]

This love is moreover the indispensable condition for guiding souls surely to God. He writes to a Mother Superior:

Try and become more and more motherly and loving.

And he adds in a happy phrase of fine psychology full of truth:

For we can govern souls by force and authority, but it is only by meekness and love that we can gain them to God.[540]

This must be an ardent but altogether supernatural love which bathes others in the Divine light and is the principle of peace:

* I do so yearn to see you give yourself without reserve to God, and find *all* in Him. The glorious Communion of Saints appeals to me more and more; we are really so "one" in Jesus Christ. The more closely we are united with Jesus, the closer the bonds of holy love embrace and envelope us. It is in Jesus and in Him *alone* that you will find those who are so dear to you in *truth*. He is Truth, and the more closely we abide in Him the *truer* is our union with those we love. If we only find them in ourselves, in our poor human hearts, in our feelings and

remembrance, our union is fruitless for them—for us, it only makes the void deeper and more hopeless. But when we unite ourselves to them in Jesus, our union is a joy for them, and peace for us.[541]

———

This love for souls is not to be had without suffering; in this domain the cross becomes even particularly heavy, but it is the secret of fecundity:

Sufferings are the price and the sign of true Divine favors... Works and foundations built upon the cross and upon sufferings are alone lasting.[542]

The sufferings you have endured are for me a sign of the special benediction of the One Who, in His wisdom, chose to found all upon *the cross.*[543]

Our Lord has given me to see that we Superiors must be united with the Good Shepherd *in His sufferings,* if we wish to do any good to the souls confided to us.[544]

These sufferings are of every kind, oftentimes anxiety concerning material difficulties weighs heavily on the shoulders of Superiors. Dom Marmion would have a great spirit of faith brought to bear in this matter. Passages such as the following abound:

Abandon yourself more and more to your Divine Spouse, "Your Father knoweth that you have need of all these things."[545] Not a hair of your head falls without His permission. Yes, He will Himself bring about your work, if you abandon yourself with all the confidence of a spouse to the *power and wisdom* of His love. The bride never gives so much pleasure and glory to her Bridegroom as when, in her difficulties, she ever keeps her eyes fixed upon Him, sure of His love, His power and His wisdom.[546]

Our Lord, in order to exercise your faith and confidence, will sometimes leave you to grapple with great temporal difficulties. But as long as you only seek Him and His will in all things, He will always come to your aid at the requisite moment. Never yield when it is a question of principle in view of a temporal advantage; if you act thus, Our Lord will always be faithful to you.[547]

He writes to another:

For what concerns your temporal affairs, I am very sorry that the question of money has turned up to worry you. But as Saint Benedict says, "if the Abbot seeks first the Kingdom of God and His justice for himself and for his children, all the rest will be added to him."[548] The weaker we are and the more incapable of helping ourselves, the more Our Lord is pleased to come to our aid. I am sure that Our Lord sends you these little worries to give you the occasion of making acts of real love and confidence.[549]

He says to a Carmelite Superioress:

A convent is a *supernatural* family depending directly for what is spiritual and what is temporal on the Heavenly Father. His protection, His fatherly providence, are in proportion to our abandon and our filial confidence. It *is impossible* that the Superior of a convent should cast herself with confidence into the Father's hands and the Heavenly Father not watch over the least things that concern her.[550]

───── ∞ ─────

Heavier sometimes, surely more painful, are difficulties and sufferings of the moral and spiritual order:

Let us labor to give ourselves to Jesus in the person of others. That admits of much interior renunciation.[551]

He concludes:

* So place yourself each day on the altar with Jesus to be offered to the glory of God and to be eaten by those around you.[552]

He writes to a religious:

I am rejoiced to hear that the Divine Master is helping you in your function as Mistress of Novices. You could not do anything more agreeable to the Sacred Heart than to fashion for Him these dear souls destined to be His intimate friends and spouses. If in this function you find the cross, know, my daughter, it is the price that a superior must pay for the choice graces necessary to her in her charge.[553]

And to a Father Master:

* It is impossible to be in charge in a monastery without having care and anxiety at times. It is part of the debt we pay to God for His protection and grace. Novices are always tempted in one way or another, but especially by false suggestions of the devil that have the appearance of good. The desire to become a Carthusian, Trappist, or worse, is quite classical as a novice's temptation. Please tell them from me that it would be most unwise after the miraculous way in which God has been leading them, to form plans etc. They should just pray "Lead kindly Light," and wait till God manifests His will. I feel convinced that He wants them to keep together, and that those who leave will find themselves *stranded*, and no longer borne on the bosom of God's grace.

You have a difficult task... Try to keep your eye fixed "ever towards the Lord, as the eyes of the handmaid are on the hands of her mistress."[554]

The ordinary, incessant cross, made all the heavier by this very continuity, is what Saint Benedict calls being under "the servitude of characters,"[555] a servitude which wears out natural energy but puts the finishing touch to patience.

Dom Marmion writes to a Superior:

Saint Paul tells us that at the moment of the Incarnation, the Sacred Humanity seeing a whole life of suffering presented by the Father, fully accepted it. "In the head of the book it is written of me that I should do Thy will. I WILL IT... Behold, I come to do Thy will, O God..." WE ARE ALL SANCTIFIED BY CHRIST'S OBEDIENCE.[556] When one accepts through obedience "to accommodate himself to a diversity of characters," it is the heaviest of crosses.[557] Saint Francis of Assisi says that, for a Superior, perfect obedience consists in this acceptance. Ever since I understood this, I have been full of joy despite many contrarieties of every kind. I see that you are going through this. Do not think of casting aside your cross like Saint Peter. *Quo vadis?*[558] It is your sanctification, especially as you did not seek it.[559]

Despite the great desire we have to do all the good and give all the pleasure in our power, it may happen that we do not know what to do for the best. If you are indulgent, others will immediately take advantage of it to get the upper hand; if you are firm, they will take the attitude of victims. And as for myself, I suffer greatly when I am not in most cordial agreement with all.[560]

He writes to a Mother Superior:

X... is your cross. You must bear with her for without that you would have the honor without the burden of superiorship.[561]

And again:

* You are carrying out God's designs by speaking plainly at times to N... She is full of good will, but also full of attachment to self-judgment and self-will. It will cost her many a pang before all that is subjected with entire suppleness to God's action. Don't be discouraged, defects which come from character are most difficult to correct, even for those who are full of good will and wish to act as they ought.[562]

For certain persons fired with zeal, there is one cross particularly hard to bear, namely that of feeling powerless before wrongdoing:

As soon as Our Lord confides souls to you, suffering is inevitable. And great is the suffering of having to witness wrongdoing which one does not succeed in suppressing. It is that of *all* those who have the charge of souls.[563]

Nevertheless, the most ardent zeal should be tempered with the most delicate discretion. Dom Marmion writes these lines all imbued with the Benedictine spirit:

Without any question, the great danger for a young Superior, however holy and enlightened she may be, is to be wanting in moderation, above all if she has an ardent and generous nature. She ought ever to have before her eyes those words of Isaiah concerning the Divine Master. "The bruised reed He shall not break, and smoking flax He shall not quench."[564] It is only when the heart becomes *incorrigible* that the words of the Holy Spirit must be followed, "Put away the evil one from you,"[565] "lest one diseased sheep should taint the whole flock."[566]

However grievous this trial may be, it must be embraced with patience for it is in the order of Providence. The soul ought to keep her gaze fixed upon Christ; she will see in Him the perfect example of the Good Shepherd:

You must keep firm and not allow these things to be spoken of. Do your duty after having taken counsel in the Heart of Jesus. Act and let others say what they will.[567]

To a Mistress of Novices:

I have been praying a great deal for you since your letter for I see that Our Lord is making you pass through the crucible. I perfectly understand your suffering, the difficulty of distinguishing between the horror and the detestation of wrong and injustice,—and your feelings towards the person herself. Our Blessed Father Saint Benedict says of the Abbot: *Oderit vitia, diligat fratres*. "Let him hate sin, and love the brethren."[568]

My daughter, Our Lord has made me understand so well recently that the perfection of obedience—for Superiors above all—consists in accepting *all the circumstances* of the sphere in which God has placed them. Jesus entering into this world was surrounded by "His brethren" who did not believe in Him and mocked at Him; by His apostles who so ill responded to His teachings and forsook Him; by the Pharisees who opposed His work and misrepresented it, etc., and He accepted *all*. "Behold I come to do Thy will."[569] He accepted it even to the last detail: "one jot, or one tittle shall not pass... till ALL be fulfilled."[570] Saint John of the Cross says that, once professed in a Community, one ought to look upon all the Sisters, all the Superiors, as so many instruments of Divine Love and Wisdom Who make "all things work together for good."[571] Let us pray much and speak little. One word can do so *much* harm![572]

On other occasions devotedness may encounter ingratitude—a deep and hidden suffering which the Divine Master knew:

I see that you are very dear to the Divine Heart of Jesus for, while confiding to you the care of His spouses, He makes you share His sufferings and humiliations. It is impossible to love Jesus truly here below without sharing His Cross, that is to say His sorrows and humiliations, and without undergoing the ingratitude of those to whom we are devoting ourselves. Those who had proclaimed Jesus on Palm Sunday, cried "Crucify Him, crucify Him" a few days later. Offer yourself every morning to Jesus at the moment of Holy Communion to serve Him the whole day in the person of each of your sisters, and then, to share His sufferings by bearing with the ingratitude of the malcontents.[573]

But where to find sustenance for this intense love of souls, where to derive that patience for every hour and sometimes for every instant, that total and constant self-abnegation? Nowhere else than in union with Jesus Christ. This union alone disperses the darkness and brings the light so indispensable to Superiors:

To be a worthy Superioress needs great purity and great elevation of intention, and it is only in very close and continual union with Our Lord, in His Heart, that one finds strength to remain thus above the influences of this earth.[574]

To a Superior he gives this warning full of faith:

If I may give you a piece of fatherly advice in the name of Jesus Christ Whose place I so unworthily hold, I would say to you, "If thy eye be single, thy whole body will be lightsome... having no part of darkness; the whole shall be lightsome, and as a bright lamp shall enlighten thee."[575] The "part of darkness" is the self-love which unconsciously seeks to attach others to oneself. Then one makes mistakes and offends and ruffles souls. I know that you have much *zeal* and *true zeal* for souls, but I believe a "part of darkness" still remains. I say this to you out of fatherly affection, and I am sure that you accept it in the spirit in which it is said, that in all things *God may be glorified.*[576]

Union with Jesus Christ is the secret of success in dealing with souls. To a Sister Superior:

One of the highest and most perfect forms of charity is that of consenting to govern others for the love of God. God has chosen you because you are so weak and little, in order that it may be clearly seen that the good you do comes from Him. "The foolishness of God is wiser than men."[577] I beg God to give you the grace to abandon yourself entirely into the hands of Jesus Christ, for when we abandon ourselves with absolute unreserved confidence to His wisdom and love, He takes a most jealous care of each detail of our life; indeed Saint Paul says "Jesus Christ is made unto us by God our wisdom, our holiness, our justice and our redemption."[578] "Reveal thy way to the Lord and He will do the rest."[579]

This union with God, with Jesus, is intensified in prayer:

Do not consider as time lost, either for yourself or *for the Community,* the moments spent, when duty so permits, in union of love with God. God is the source of *all* the good that you do in yourself or in others.[580]

Let others pray for you, but your prayer is your love. God knows better than you what is best for you and what is best for the Community. The more your faith increases, the more confidence you will have in the Sacred Humanity wherewith you are so *united* through the Holy Eucharist. That is the way for you. Christ will take you with Him into the bosom of the Trinity. There you will be in the truth, and in light and love.[581]

It is natural that he should develop this theme, because in it he reveals unawares the result of his own experience. He writes to a Carmelite Prioress:

Unite yourself more and more to Jesus Christ, so that He may act through you.

1. He is the Son of God; He is altogether *ad Patrem*, for the Father; He attributes to the Father all that He is and all that He has, "all My things are Thine";[582]

2. He is Eternal Wisdom; He glorifies His Father in communicating this Wisdom to those whom the Father gives Him;

3. He is *Sapientia spirans amorem*, Wisdom breathing love: the Holy Spirit proceeds from Him. You should then unite yourself to Him in all this, for you hold His place towards those whom He has confided to you.[583]

He writes to another Prioress of Carmel:

Our Lord will do great things for you on three conditions:

1. That you habitually keep yourself very small in His presence, without any pretension or looking upon yourself.

2. That you always lean upon Jesus Christ, for He is *the Way*: "I am the Way... *no man* cometh to the Father, but by Me."[584]

3. That you lay your soul open to the rays of the Sun of Justice that so He may sanctify you in truth.[585]

More than one of these letters are addressed to Mistresses of Novices. A particularly delicate mission is that of forming young souls to a life of union with Jesus Christ. Dom Marmion takes special satisfaction in speaking of it. Read these lines revealing such a high and supernatural viewpoint:

The charge of a mistress of novices is a very beautiful one. If you think you are able to do anything for souls by yourself it will not succeed, "for without Me you can do nothing,"[586] but if you cleave closely to God all will go well, because Our Lord will then inspire you Himself as to what you ought to do and say. Our Lord has chosen you to be His aid; your mission is to lead souls to Him, to prepare them for the nuptials with the Spouse. Saint Bernardine of Siena says that all those who, by obedience, receive the charge of souls ought to count upon the help of God Who is bound to enlighten and inspire them. You have received a divine mandate. God binds Himself to give you His graces and lights, and you should have faith in these lights and believe that they come to you from the Holy Spirit.

On the day of your confirmation, Jesus, in the person of the Bishop, imprinted the sign of the cross upon your soul like a seal, *Signo te signo Crucis,* I sign thee with the sign of the Cross. This sign remains upon your soul; the Holy Spirit continually sees this seal as a title to His graces. I want your soul to become more and more the sanctuary of the Holy Spirit from which a ray of God escapes upon the souls with whom you enter into contact.

But, for that, it is necessary for you to disappear, for you to renounce your own ideas, your little personal methods, so as to let Christ act fully in you and through you. If each morning you remit yourself into His hands, He will act through you. A holy religious whom Our Lord Himself directs, for she is a missionary, told me that being very quick-witted she had wished to take all the initiative in a certain transaction. She heard Our Lord say to her, "It is for you to choose: either it is to be Me to do it without you, or you without Me." She understood and left the matter to one of her sisters. Our Lord did not wish her to act by herself.

If when you have done your very best, things do not succeed, don't be astonished; look at Jesus, see how much was still wanting to His apostles, see their attitude during the Passion. This point of view will console you.[587]

He blends counsels of discretion with the most supernatural views:

It is a sign of the special love of Jesus for you to have entrusted the novices to you. He asks Saint Peter, "Lovest thou Me more than these," and as reward, He gives him His sheep.

1. Lead them to God through Jesus Christ. He is *the only Way*. "I am the Way... *no man* cometh to the Father, but by Me."

2. As you have robust health, try to understand that what is a trifle for you is difficult for the weak. This is very important.

3. Set *no limit* to your abandon to God. As soon as you make any exception, you are no longer *one* with God and peace departs. It would be preferring your little ideas to those of God Whose love is infinite and wisdom boundless. He loves those you love and better than you do. The more you count upon Him, the more He will be the Shepherd and the Father of the flock. He said to Mary, *Unum est necessarium*. "But one thing is necessary," and we offer Him an affront in thinking that any creature is necessary to His works. This does not at all prevent your praying with all your heart, as I do, that God will spare you this chalice.[588] During your mental prayer be altogether His without concerning yourself with anything else. He will take care of you if you think of Him.[589]

Again read these counsels, bearing the mark of such profound wisdom, to another mistress of novices, a Carmelite:

As for the *interior* formation of novices, nothing is of obligation except that the *novice mistress* should have a great knowledge of the spirit and doctrine of Saint Teresa which, insensibly and without her suspecting it, will shine out in the way she understands holiness, the Scriptures, etc. It is not so much the words nor passages from the writings of your holy Mother which will be useful for the novices (later they will be able to draw upon this rich treasury of the mystical life, also in Saint John of the Cross), but what is important is that the mistress of novices should see things from the same special angle as she who is called Teresa OF JESUS.[590]

It is then the spirit of Jesus which is to animate the mistress of novices in her important mission. To live by this spirit and to make those under her charge live by it, is the sum total of her work. This thought inspires Dom Marmion with a beautiful development:

I am so happy to see that Our dear Savior gives you His Spirit. Yes, indeed, in the direction of souls and especially of beginners, we must often await the moment of grace, and know how to bear upon our shoulders these poor little sheep still so weak and tired out by their small efforts. You must know, my daughter, that these words of Jesus, "Without Me, you can do nothing," were said above all and before all, of the efforts we make for the sanctification of souls, and that it is above all by *your* union with Jesus, by *your* immolation to His love that grace is given to your children. Saint John of the Cross says that one act of pure love of God does more for the salvation of souls than any exterior works. Try above all to act in such a way that your novices learn to do all for love. To do one's duty is a great thing, but to do one's duty out of love is greater still. Those who act first of all out of a sense of duty, and in the second place out of love, will always be wanting in something indefinable which draws down God's look upon them. The best way is to perform the duty as perfectly as possible, not for the esteem we have for it (that would only be moral virtue), but because the performance of the duty is the expression of love: "If you love Me, keep My commandments."[591]

Here then, as moreover everywhere, love, the summing up of all, is shown by deeds:

Without being severe, perhaps you would do well to demand great exactitude for all that concerns your customs and holy traditions. Fidelity is the flower of love, to which nothing is little. Saint Teresa said that she would give her life for the least rubric or for the least point of her rule, for she saw in it the expression of the good pleasure of her Beloved.[592]

Fidelity is the flower of love to which nothing is little.

Could we close these pages better than with this delicate thought, so true, and so happily expressed![593]

At the conclusion of this treatise on the life of union with God we cannot do better than again ask Dom Marmion himself to give us a summary of his admirable doctrine: he does so in a few lines which reveal once again that ardent love for Christ and souls which was the one passion of his whole life:

A tending towards God in Himself with a sense of confusion at our unworthiness and confidence in His goodness and in the Precious Blood of Jesus Christ are the three notes of *real* union with God. Do not fear. This way is *sure*. Nothing glorifies God so much as the triumph of His grace in a soul that acknowledges her misery, her weakness, her unworthiness, and that hopes for *all* from His power and His goodness. This is the "praise of the glory of His grace" of which Saint Paul speaks.[594]

Notes

INTRODUCTION

1. Archbishop Goodier refers here to Dom Raymond Thibaut's biography, *Abbot Columba Marmion, A Master of the Spiritual Life, 1858–1923* (St. Louis, Mo.: B. Herder, 1942) [hereinafter *"Abbot Columba Marmion"*]. It is to Thibaut that Goodier's Introduction is addressed.

PREFACE

2. *Abbot Columba Marmion*, chap. XI, "The Spiritual Director." See also chap. X, "Christ's Representative," and chap. XIV, "Christ's Apostle."

3. Ibid., p. 271.

4. Is this not also Bossuet's method? "You often distress yourself," the great bishop wrote to one under his direction, "in saying that I do not reply concerning certain matters to which I feel I have replied, because I lay down a principle whereby one can give oneself the reply, which is a way of replying often useful to employ, because by it the soul learns to consult within herself the eternal truth, that is to say, to listen to this truth." One of the reasons for this method is that Bossuet, following the bent of his genius, is more concerned with man in general, than with the individual. Hence, the wide, liberal, and disinterested character that we find in his direction. We likewise find these traits in that of Dom Marmion. We know the Abbot of Maredsous read Bossuet's works with pleasure.

5. Expression of Saint Benedict designating the faith. Prologue of *The Rule of St. Benedict* [hereinafter *"Rule"*].

6. Saint Francis de Sales, letter to the Duke de Bellegarde.

7. *Abbot Columba Marmion*, p. 248.

8. *Lettres spirituelles de saint Anselme* (Paris, 1925). Introduction XXXIX.

9. *Christ, the Ideal of the Monk* (St. Louis, Mo.: B. Herder, 1926), p. viii.

10. Exception made in part of the last two chapters, and several other places dealing with direction given in particular cases.

11. There are some of Dom Marmion's correspondents with whom we have not been able to get in touch. Therefore, we venture to ask them, if their eyes chance to fall on these lines, kindly to transmit to us any copy, entire or in part, of Dom Marmion's letters; we shall be most grateful to them.

12. This publication had already been decided upon at the time when Dom Marmion's biography appeared in December 1929. We have had to take up our work again, in consequence of the belated communication of an important collection of letters; secondly we have had to wait, more than a year, for the communication, promised at different times, of numerous letters which we knew to be of great interest, and which unhappily are not yet forthcoming.

13. We have left many of Dom Marmion's letters intact; by too frequent subdividing somewhat of the vigor of the thought would have been lost. In a work of this character certain repetitions are inevitable. We have left them. Moreover to have suppressed them would have been to destroy the harmony of their development, and at the same time to weaken the persuasive force of their reasoning.

CHAPTER ONE

14. *Abbot Columba Marmion*, pp. 270-271.

15. January 8, 1908. This idea of the three spirits is already to be met with among Dom Marmion's personal notes; it is dated Pentecost, 1907. See *Abbot Columba Marmion*, chap. VIII, "Graces of Union," pp. 165-166.

16. Cf. Genesis 2:17 and 3:4.

17. "Justus meus ex fide vivit." Hebrews 10:38.

18. Cf. Matthew 7:16.

19. The Hebrew name "Michael" literally means "Who is like unto God."

20. Cf. John 14:26.

21. December 1, 1922; Dom Marmion died on the following January 30.

22. 2 John 1:4.

23. "Ego sum Veritas." Cf. John 14:6.

24. "Quaerite faciem ejus semper." Psalm 104:4. [Nota Bene: Citations to the Psalms follow the numbering of the Douay-Rheims.]

25. "Peccatum meum contra me est SEMPER." Psalm 50:5.

26. "Non intres in judicium cum servo tuo, Domine." Psalm 142:2.

27. "Et REPLEBIT Eum spiritus timoris Domini." Isaiah 11:3.

28. May 1, 1918.

29. "Quomodo miseretur pater filiorum, misertus est Dominus timentibus se, QUONIAM IPSE COGNOVIT FIGMENTUM NOSTRUM." Psalm 102:13.

30. "Libenter gloriabor in infirmitatibus meis ut inhabitet in me virtus Christi." 2 Corinthians 12:9.

31. "Non enim accepistis spiritum servitutis iterum in timore, sed accepistis spiritum ADOPTIONIS filiorum, in quo clamamus, Abba Pater." Romans 8:15.

32. November 15, 1908.

33. October 15, 1920.

34. January 12, 1912.

35. "Non habens ullam partem tenebrarum." Luke 11:36.

36. May 8, 1913.

37. "RESPICE FINEM, et omnia quaecumque facies prosperabuntur." Cf. Psalm 1:3. Letter dated December 4, 1912.

38. December 4, 1917.

39. January 23, 1918.

40. May 1914.

41. January 4, 1914.

42. November 7, 1917.

43. April 22, 1906.

44. John 8:25.

45. October 26, 1911.

46. April 30, 1906.

47. "Ego ero tecum." Exodus 3:12. Letter dated July 27, 1912.

48. April 23, 1913.

49. Word illegible.

CHAPTER TWO

50. *Abbot Columba Marmion*, pp. 65 ff.

51. "This is the general rule of our obedience written in large hand, namely we must do all by love and nothing by force." October 14, 1604.

52. April 3, 1903.

53. January 21, 1913.

54. October 21, 1908.

55. "Cooperabitur in bonum." Romans 8:28. Letter dated January 3, 1904.

56. February 13, 1904.

57. January 3, 1906.

58. 1905, without other date.

59. November 20, 1906.

60. January 24, 1904.

61. "Et plenitudine ejus nos omnes accepimus." John 1:16. Letter dated November 30, 1920.

62. September 18, 1922.

63. Matthew 12:50.

64. June 9, 1903.

65. There is scarcely need to say that for Dom Marmion as for every moralist, the first source of morality is the goodness of the action itself, considered in its conformity with the Divine law; but speaking to souls that seek God, and whose actions have habitually this essential goodness, Dom Marmion had to insist with good reason upon purity of motives of action.

66. "Dilexit me et tradidit semetipsum pro me." Galatians 2:20.

67. "Impendam et superimpendar." 2 Corinthians 12:15.

68. "Ubi amatur non laboratur." Saint Augustine, *Confessions*.

69. About 1920.

70. Undated.

71. "Pater non reliquit Me solum, quia quae placita sunt ei facio semper." John 8:29.

72. Undated.

73. March 6, 1901.

74. Cf. Luke 11:34.

75. November 13, 1901.

76. December 3, 1921.

77. The letter of the Sacred Congregation of Rites authorizing the Bishop of Bayeux to set the procedure on foot by the examination of the writings of the Servant of God is dated February 30, 1910; the first session of the informative process dates from the month of August 1910. In June 1914, the favorable sentence of the Sacred Congregation of Rites terminated the informative process.

78. "Estote perfecti sicut et Pater vester caelestis perfectus est." Matthew 5:48.

79. Cf. *Christ in His Mysteries,* conference, "The Heart of Christ," § 3.

80. Undated.

81. Cf. Galatians 2:20.

82. "Ipse labor amatur." Saint Augustine, *Confessions.*

83. April 10, 1903.

84. August 16, 1904.

85. November 27, 1903.

86. January 29, 1907.

87. December 27, 1906. "Da nobis, quaesumus, omnipotens Deus: ut qui nova Incarnati Verbi tui luce perfundimur: hoc in nostro resplendeat opere, quod per fidem fulget in mente."

88. Undated.

89. Undated.

90. November 21, 1900.

91. March 29, 1920.

92. "Nam et si ambulavero in medio umbrae mortis, non timebo mala, quoniam TU mecum es." Psalm 22:4.

93. Undated.

94. "Majorem horum non habes gratiam quam ut audiam filias meas in veritate ambulare." 3 John 1:4. This same thought is found in a letter written to another nun, ten years later (December 27, 1916); and see above, p. 6, text accompanying note 22.

95. Revelation 3:15, 16.

96. March 7, 1907.

97. *Christ, the Ideal of the Monk,* p. 146.

98. Undated.

99. *Christ, the Ideal of the Monk,* pp. 139 ff.

100. December 5, 1894.

101. September 12, 1613 (*Œuvres*).

102. "...Nos Unigeniti (Filii Dei) nova per carnem Nativitas liberet, quos sub peccati jugo vetusta servitus tenet." Collect for the Third Mass on Christmas Day.

103. *Bluestockings,* i.e., pedantry. Refers to the nickname of a women's literary club of 18th-century London.

104. "Inquire pacem et persequere eam." Psalm 33:15.

105. September 21, 1920.

106. December 24, 1917.

107. Good Friday, 1895.

108. May 1, 1918.

109. May 26, 1914. "I leave you liberty of spirit," wrote Saint Francis de Sales to Madame de Chantal, "not that which stops obedience, for that is the liberty of the flesh, but that which stops constraint and scruple, or overeagerness. I want you to understand that if you have a great love for obedience and submission, and yet happen to omit your spiritual exercises, which may be for you a kind of obedience, this omission may be supplied by love." October 14th, 1604 (*Œuvres*).

110. February 20, 1917.

111. Dom Ryelandt, *Essai sur la physionomie morale de Saint Benoît.*

112. "In sinu Patris." John 1:18.

113. March 6, 1914.

114. "Christus factus est NOBIS sapientia a Deo et justitia et SANCTIFICATIO et redemptio." 1 Corinthians 1:30.

115. "Praedestinavit nos Deus conformes fieri imaginis Filii sui." Romans 8:29.

116. "Hic est Filius meus dilectus in quo mihi complacui." Matthew 3:17.

117. "Lapis angularis faciens utraque unum." From the Antiphon "O Rex Gentium..." December 22. Cf. Ephesians 2:14. Dom Marmion uses this text here in its applied sense.

118. "Ego sum vitis, vos palmites." John 15:5. Cf. Concil. Trident, sess. VI, c. 7.

119. "Quoniam estis filii misit Spiritum Filii sui in corda vestra clamantem: Abba, Pater." Galatians 4:6.

120. "Spiritus est qui vivificat." 2 Corinthians 3:6.

121. July 18, 1917.

122. "Ego sum ostium." John 10:7.

123. "Unigenitus qui est in sinu Patris, ipse enarravit." John 1:18.

124. "Non enim judicavi me scire aliquid inter vos, nisi Jesum Christum et hunc crucifixum." 1 Corinthians 2:2.

125. April 9, 1903.

126. May 17, 1903.

127. He writes to a nun: "You are in the right way for you are in *the Way*. The more we believe in the power of the Sacred Humanity of Jesus to lead us even into the *Sinus Patris* [Bosom of the Father], and the more strong our faith in Jesus Christ, the more it honors God."

128. Cf. John 15:5-7.

129. Cf. 1 Corinthians 1:30.

130. March 14, 1902.

131. Dom Marmion does not here mean *personality* in the merely psychological sense as modern philosophers often understand it. Christ, in fact, had His integral human "conscience" and will. But His divinity and His humanity were two distinct natures of a single being, of a single Person. From this mysterious oneness and from the Beatific Vision which it involved for the soul of Jesus was derived the absolute impossibility of discord between these two wills, the divine and the human. His soul's moral harmony had then its source in the absence with Him of human personality (in its ontological meaning and even to a certain point in its psychological meaning).

    What for Christ was *ontological* necessity may, with man, be won by *moral* effort: the habitual conformity with God's will may be legitimately called (although by analogy) virtuous abandonment of one's own "personality" in the depreciatory—but alas! very real— sense of this word. This depreciatory sense of the word personality ought to be understood of all that is disordered in attachment to self; the cult of personal ideas, self-will, the seeking after self-exaltation apart from God. This is the whole meaning of the extracts we give here and in the following pages. Under Dom Marmion's pen the word personality, with the creature, is taken in the order of *activity* (knowledge, love, deeds), for in the order of *being,* we keep our personality. This distinction is familiar to him.

    See notably *Christ, the Life of the Soul,* conference "Christ Model of Perfection," § IV; *Christ in His Mysteries,* conference "The Word made Flesh," end of § III; *Christ, the Ideal of the Monk,* chap. X, §§ IV and V; *Sponsa Verbi,* p. 32, note; *Abbot Columba Marmion,* p. 409, n. 2.

132. Idea inspired by the *Rule* of Saint Benedict: "To dash against Christ our evil thoughts." Prologue and chap. IV.

133. September 8, 1920.

134. September 21, 1910

135. "Ut jumentum factus sum apud te: ad nihilum redactus sum et nescivi." Psalm 72:22-23.

136. "Christus mihi vita." Cf. Philippians 1:21.

137. "Ut inveniar in Illo." Philippians 3:9.

138. See discussion note 131, above.

139. Undated.

140. "Pater non reliquit me solum qui quae placita sunt ei facio semper." Cf. John 8:29.

141. Cf. John 14:23.

142. 1907, without other date.

143. Cf. Matthew 11:27.

144. December 1913.

145. Cf. John 3:30.

146. October 21, 1900.

147. "Semper apparet vultui Dei pro nobis." Hebrews 9:24.

148. December 30, 1912.

149. December 5, 1919. See the development of this thought in *Christ, the Life of the Soul*, conference, "Baptism," and in *Christ in His Mysteries*, conference, "Si consurrexistis cum Christo."

150. January 15, 1901.

151. "Et quicumque hanc regulam secuti fuerint pax super illos et misericordia." Galatians 6:16.

152. Undated.

153. Cf. Colossians 2:3.

154. November 19, 1910.

155. 1906.

156. Dom Marmion is evidently speaking here of the difficulty inherent to the deed itself that has to be done. This difficulty is blended with the goodness of the deed and it is then the source of the greatest merit; it testifies in fact, when one overcomes it, to a greater *actual* charity. The difficulty that comes from unfavorable subjective dispositions, far from being a source of merit, is only too often the sign of mediocre love.

157. November 21, 1900.

158. March 28, 1904.

159. October 4, 1900.

160. "Quaerite faciem eius semper." Psalm 104:4. Letter undated.

161. "Mala sua praeterita cun gemitu et lacrymis QUOTIDIE in oratione Deo confiteri." *Rule*, chap. IV, 58.

162. "Hoc enim sentite in vobis quod et in Christo Jesu." Philippians 2:5.

163. "Nemo venit ad Patrem nisi per Me." John 14:6.

164. "Ego sum via." Ibid.

165. "Per Ipsum, et cum Ipso et in Ipso OMNIS honor et gloria Deo Patri." Canon of the Mass.

166. "Delicias non amplecti." *Rule*, chap. IV, 12.

CHAPTER THREE

167. See the development of these ideas in *Christ, the Life of the Soul,* conference, "Our Supernatural Growth in Christ."

168. Cf. Philippians 3:20.

169. "Funes ceciderunt mihi in praeclaris." Psalm 15:6.

170. Dom Marmion had already made an extract of this passage in his private notebook in 1897 (cf. *Abbot Columba Marmion*, p. 109). This thought "of one of the greatest mystics of the Order of Saint Benedict," as he calls Blois (May 29, 1915), must have "struck" Marmion vividly, for he frequently quotes it in a succession of his letters from 1902 to 1922 to encourage souls to pursue the great work of their sanctification valiantly.

171. *Spiritual Canticle,* strophe XXIX. We come across this citation also in an agenda of 1900, dated November 24, feast of Saint John of the Cross, etc.

172. November 19, 1902. See likewise a letter of March 4, 1907, on p. 67-69.

173. "Illam tibi perfice munus aeternum." Cf. Secret of the Mass for Trinity Sunday.

174. "Ego principium qui et loquor vobis." Cf. John 8:25.

175. November 29, 1920.

176. August 16, 1904.

177. October 14, 1917.

178. July 2, 1913.

179. February 10, 1914.

180. "Haec est voluntas Dei, sanctificatio vestra." 1 Thessalonians 4:3.

181. "Sine Me NIHIL potestis facere." John 15:5.

182. "Sive parum, sive multum, sine illo fieri non potest sine quo nihil fieri potest." Saint Augustine, *Treatise on Saint John,* LXXXI.

183. *Christ, the Life of the Soul,* chap. III, § 4.

184. October 26, 1917.

185. November 20, 1909.

186. "A fructibus eorum cognoscetis eos." Matthew 7:16.

187. Luke 10:21.

188. January 10, 1907.

189. March 6, 1907.

190. Undated.

191. May 1, 1915.

192. June 27, 1915.

193. May 21, 1895.

194. April 20, 1922.

195. "Ecce nos reliquimus omnia et secuti sumus te," "Behold we have left all things, and have followed Thee." Matthew 19:27.

196. Prologue of the *Rule*.

197. "Misericordia Domini plena est terra." Psalm 32:5.

198. "Deus, propitius esto mihi peccatori." Luke 18:13.

199. Undated.

200. November 20, 1914. The stability and fecundity of works depend on the cross. "Works, and above all foundations, built upon the cross are alone lasting." January 23, 1909.

201. May 28, the year not given.

202. Out of discretion we do not give the date.

203. September 16, 1921.

204. December 18, 1916.

205. December 12, 1909.

206. "Ex imis praecordiis."

207. "Qui facit peccatum, servus est peccati." John 8:34.

208. "Qui amat creaturam, servus est creaturae." 1902. Out of discretion, we only give the date of the year.

209. "Christus, unctus, consecratus, vivens propter Patrem."

210. 1907.

211. June 17, 1902.

212. February 24, 1921.

213. "Patientia opus perfectum habet." James 1:4.

214. Prologue of the *Rule*. Letter dated July 11, 1922.

215. September 17, 1894.

216. 1895.

217. "Abominatio Domino est omnis arrogans." Proverbs 16:5.

218. December 15, 1894.

219. January 13, 1895.

220. February 25, 1895.

221. March 19, 1895. A short time afterwards, this spiritual daughter of Dom Marmion entered a Benedictine cloister where he had often the opportunity of seeing her which put an end to the correspondence. There is still one undated note (probably about 1903) where in reference to a niece of his correspondent who had just joined her in religion, Dom Marmion wrote to her jokingly, "I hope at all events that she will turn out better than her aunt who, despite all the help and trouble one may give oneself to sanctify her, still always remains so cowardly. But Our Lord is all powerful and I am confident that we shall arrive at something in the end." This religious was for a long time to edify her community by her ardent charity and to die like a saint.

222. August 31, 1902.

223. December 2, 1902.

224. November 1906. This note is written in pencil. Dom Marmion wrote it from his bed in the clinic where he was lying after an operation.

225. Cf. Sirach (Ecclesiasticus) 18:16, 17; *Rule*, chap. XXXI.

226. "Adimpleo in corpore meo quae desunt passionum Christi pro corpore ejus quod est Ecclesia." Colossians 1:24.

227. 1 Corinthians 12:27.

228. December 6, 1906.

229. This is the thought of Dom Pie de Hemptinne, one of the holiest of Dom Marmion's spiritual sons: "When a soul is united to God, He pursues her, He persecutes her in order to possess her. How I have felt that!" *Une âme bénédictine*, p. 97.

230. Cf. *Sponsa Verbi*, chap. I and following.

231. Cf. John 15:1-2.

232. March 4, 1907. "Say to yourself that you entered the convent to be fashioned like a stone that is hewn and made to fit into a building. With this idea in mind, you will look upon all your fellow religious as workmen whom God has placed near you to hew and perfect you by mortification." *Advice to a religious*. Sequel to *The Ascent to Mount Carmel*.

233. Cf. Exodus 4:25 ("Immediately Sephora took a very sharp stone, and circumcised the foreskin of her son, and touched his [Moses'] feet, and said: 'A bloody spouse art thou to me.'") (Douay-Rheims).

234. "Libenter gloriabor in infirmitatibus meis UT inhabitet in me VIRTUS Christi." 2 Corinthians 12:9.

235. "In hoc clarificatus est Pater meus ut FRUCTUM PLURIMUM afferatis; qui manet in Me et Ego in eo, hic fert fructum multum." John 15:8, 5. Letter dated March 15, 1914.

236. In April 1905, at the age of sixteen. According to the testimony of all who knew her hers was a soul radiant with innocence and high ideals.

237. Allusion to the entry of a sister at Carmel and to the death of a young brother in February 1903.

238. Correspondence was suspended in the monastery during the Lenten season, but Dom Marmion's delicate and supernatural charity relaxed the rigidity of this principle in favor of one of Christ's suffering members.

239. *Alpargates*: the special sandals worn by Carmelites; *togue*: the small cap worn under the veil. [Translator's note.]

240. "Deus qui in assumptae carnis infirmitate jacentem mundum erexisti." Dom Marmion here combines in a single phrase the substance of two different collects: the one for the Second Sunday after Easter, the other for the Feast of the Lance and Nails.

241. May 16, 1915.

242. "Vere languores nostros ipse tulit et dolores nostros ipse portavit." Isaiah 53:4.

243. "In similitudinem carnis peccati." Romans 8:3.

244. Revelation 2:23.

245. "Desiderium pauperum exaudivit auris tua." Psalm 9:17.

246. "Patientia vobis NECESSARIA est." Hebrews 10:36.

247. From discretion we do not give the date.

248. "In aeternum misericordia aedificabitur in caelis." Cf. Psalm 88:3.

249. "Vere languores nostros ipse tulit et dolores nostros ipse portavit." Isaiah 53:4.

250. "Per PATIENTIAM passionibus Christi PARTICIPAMUS." Prologue of the *Rule*.

251. Out of discretion we do not give the date. See the same thought in a letter of December 22, 1922, in *Abbot Columba Marmion*, p. 469.

252. March 29, 1920.

253. November 1, 1921.

254. December 14, 1921.

255. June 24, 1919.

256. October 18, 1921.

257. "Quod infirmum est Dei fortius est hominibus." 1 Corinthians 1:25.

258. "Passionibus Christi per patientiam participamus."

259. November 21, 1922.

260. "Sponsabo te mihi in fide." Hosea 2:19.

261. November 21, 1922.

CHAPTER FOUR

262. Cf. Saint John of the Cross.

263. April 9, 1918.

264. Romans 1:17; Hebrews 10:38. Cf. *Christ, the Life of the Soul,* Book II, chap. I, "Faith, Foundation of the Christian Life."

265. Cf. *Abbot Columba Marmion,* pp. 380 ff.

266. January 1, 1920.

267. January 10, 1907.

268. March 1907.

269. April 19, 1909.

270. Undated.

271. November 20, 1922.

272. Undated.

273. October 4, 1913.

274. December 26, 1916.

275. Undated.

276. November 13, 1917.

277. April 19, 1906.

278. December 7, 1916, to a missionary nun.

279. October 26, 1917, to a nun.

280. November 21, 1922, to a Benedictine nun.

281. "Sponsabo te mihi in fide." Hosea 2:20.

282. 1909, without other date; to a Carmelite.

283. *Thabor,* i.e., Mount Thabor, where Christ's Transfiguration took place. Letter dated February 14, 1914.

284. January 29, the year not given.

285. Tobit 12:13.

286. December 27, 1913.

287. December 31, 1919.

288. "Nubes et caligo in circuitu ejus." Psalm 96:2.

289. "Domine bonum est nos hic esse." Matthew 17:4-8.

290. "Sine fide impossibile placere Deo." Hebrews 11:6.

291. 1 John 4:16.

292. Psalm 67.

293. "Non fuerunt MEMORES multitudinis misericordiae suae." Cf. Psalm 105:7.

294. "Semper hi errant corde." Cf. Psalm 94:10.

295. March 7, 1909.

296. June 15, 1921.

297. Without exact date; about February 1920.

298. January 10, 1907.

299. November 5, 1906.

300. 1 John 1:5.

301. January 12, 1918.

302. November 30, 1921.

303. "Misereor super turbam." Mark 8:2.

304. "Beatus qui intelligit super egenum et pauperem." Psalm 40:2.

305. Undated.

306. Undated.

307. Undated.

308. Undated.

309. "Libenter gloriabor in infirmitatibus meis ut habitet in me virtus Christi." 2 Corinthians 12:9. Letter not dated.

310. Undated.

311. Undated.

312. Undated.

313. Undated.

314. "Dominus mortificat et vivificat, deducit ad inferos et reducit." 1 Samuel 2:6.

315. May 1, 1915.

316. "Ego Sum Principium qui et loquor vobis." John 8:25.

317. "Bonum aliquid in se cum viderit Deo applicet, non sibi." *Rule*, chap. IV, 42.

318. "Sine tuo numine, nihil est in homine." Sequence *Veni Sancte Spiritus*.

319. January 19, 1905.

320. September 29, 1915.

321. "MAXIME miseranda et parcendo." Collect for the Tenth Sunday after Pentecost.

322. "Abyssus abyssum invocat."

323. Undated, after 1916. See *Abbot Columba Marmion*, pp. 419 ff.

324. Psalm 104:4. Letter dated April 19, 1920.

325. January 13, 1895.

326. "Beatus vir qui suffert tentationem." James 1:12.

327. Sexagesima. Cf. 2 Corinthians 12.

328. February 16, 1903.

329. July 14, 1909.

330. Cf. Romans 4:18.

331. September 20, 1909.

332. Cf. Psalm 144:8.

333. "Factus est nobis sapientia a Deo et justitia el sanctificatio et redemptio." 1 Corinthians 1:30.

334. See the development of this thought in *Abbot Columba Marmion*, pp. 394 ff.

335. "Vere languores nostros ipse tulit." Isaiah 53:4.

336. "Beatus qui intelligit super egenum et pauperem." Cf. Psalm 40:2.

337. June 22, 1918.

338. "Vere languores nostros ipse tulit et dolores nostros ipse portavit. Posuit in eo Dominus iniquitatem omnium nostrum." Isaiah 53:4, 6.

339. "Factus est pro nobis peccatum." 2 Corinthians 5:21.

340. "Libenter gloriabor in infirmitatibus meis ut inhabitet in me virtus Christi." 2 Corinthians 12:9.

341. "Laeva ejus sub capite meo et dextera ejus amplexabitur me." Canticles 2:6. Letter not dated.

342. July 1, 1915.

343. "Libenter gloriabor in infirmitatibus meis." 2 Corinthians 12:9.

344. "Vos estis corpus Christi et membra de membro." 1 Corinthians 12:27.

345. December 30, 1904.

346. "Nos credidimus caritati Dei." Cf. 1 John 4:16.

347. November 30, 1920.

348. June 5, the year not given.

349. November 29, 1906.

350. Cf. 1 John 4:12.

351. September 1, 1909.

352. June 5, 1916.

353. Holy Saturday, 1922.

354. "In SOLA spe gratiae caelestis innititur " Collect for the Fifth Sunday after the Epiphany. Letter dated March 14, 1914.

355. January 2, 1922.

356. In 1918.

357. See Chapter II § 1.

358. Undated.

359. "Abnegare semetipsum sibi ut sequatur Christum." *Rule* of Saint Benedict, chap. IV, 10.

360. June 12, 1906.

361. 1906.

362. October 8, the year not given, but about 1896.

363. "His qui diligunt Deum omnia cooperantur in bonum." Romans 8:28.

364. November 30, 1920.

365. July 10, 1917.

366. "Nisi efficiamini sicut parvuli non intrabitis in regnum coelorum." Matthew 18:3.

367. "Jacta super Dominum curam tuam, et ipse te enutriet." Psalm 54:23 Letter dated December 11, 1900.

368. "Maledictus homo qui confidit in homine." Jeremiah 17:5.

369. "Dominus dedit, Dominus abstulit, sit nomen Domini benedictum." Job 1:21.

370. John 17:10.

371. Psalm 44:15.

372. April 3, 1908.

373. June 24, 1917.

374. February 8, 1909.

375. As is shown by the context, this evidently concerns *extraordinary* signs.

376. October 25, 1917.

377. "Sollicitus es tu et turbaris erga plurima, porro unum est necessarium." Luke 10:41-42.

378. December 27, 1915.

379. "Patientia opus perfectum habet." James 1:4.

380. "Passionibus Christi per patientian participamus." Prologue of the *Rule*. Letter dated July 11, 1922.

381. March 14, 1914.

382. "Haec est hora vestra et POTESTAS TENEBRARUM." Luke 22:53.

383. "Vere languores nostros ipse tulit." Isaiah 52:4.

384. April 27, 1922.

385. June 21, 1920.

386. June 9, 1917. See in *Abbot Columba Marmion*, pp. 244 ff., numerous extracts of the same kind.

387. July 31, 1917.

388. Psalm 9:17.

389. April 28, 1908.

390. March 24, 1916.

391. March 14, 1902.

392. Cf. Matthew 22:37-39; Mark 12:30-31; Luke 10:27.

393. Cf. *Christ, the Life of the Soul*, chap. XI, "Love One Another." See also the conference on "Good Zeal" in *Christ, the Ideal of the Monk*.

394. Undated, but about 1901.

395. "Ut unum sint, sicut Ego in Te et Tu in Me, ut sint consummati in unum." John 17:21. Letter dated May 26, 1908.

396. Cf. Matthew 25:40.

397. December 17, 1901.

398. November 19, 1902.

399. Luke 10:42.

400. December 4, 1919.

401. John 11:36.

402. July 7, 1920.

403. 1908.

404. John 12:24.

405. May 7, 1914.

406. October 4, 1913.

407. November 27, the year not given, but about 1903.

408. Same date.

409. Cf. Matthew 25:40.

410. April 3, 1903.

411. June 9, 1903.

412. November 27, 1894.

413. Cf. Matthew 7:1-2.

414. November 30, 1920.

415. Undated.

416. "A fructibus eorum cognoscetis eos..." Matthew 7:16. Letter dated February 8, 1901.

417. "Vere languores nostros ipse tulit et dolores nostros ipse portavit." Isaiah 53:4.

418. "Rogo, Pater, ut omnes unum sint, sicut Tu in Me et Ego in Te, ut sint consummati in unum." John 17:21.

419. "Date et dabitur vobis; mensuram bonam et coagitatam et super-effluentem dabunt in sinum vestrum." Luke 6:38.

420. "Viam mandatorum tuorum cucurri cum dilatasti cor meum." Psalm 118:32. Letter dated February 3, 1904.

CHAPTER FIVE

421. To these must be added the chapter "Spiritus Precum" in *Abbot Columba Marmion*, pp. 424 ff.

422. The greater number, we say, for in some of these written to people in the world are to be found directions suitable to their state.

423. November 2, 1915.

424. Collect *ad postulandam gratiam Spiritus Sancti*. Letter dated May 29, 1915.

425. December 1, 1916.

426. November 7, 1917.

427. May 28, the year not given.

428. *Christ, the Life of the Soul,* chap. "Prayer"; *Christ, the Ideal of the Monk,* chap. "Monastic Prayer."

429. Cf. John 14:23.

430. Undated.

431. "Exardescet ignis." Psalm 38:4.

432. Undated.

433. November 2, 1915.

434. October 17, 1891.

435. January 29, the year not given.

436. See *Abbot Columba Marmion*, pp. 89 ff.

437. November 21, 1922.

438. Cf. Sirach (Ecclesiasticus) 39:6. Letter dated August 5, 1917.

439. By a slip of the pen Dom Marmion connects under the same title two different works of Bossuet, but from his oral teaching it may be concluded that he especially means the *Méditations sur l'Évangile*.

440. June 5, 1916.

441. December 5, 1894.

442. November 10, 1917.

443. December 22, 1916.

444. "Quaerite Dominum, quaerite faciem ejus SEMPER." Cf. Psalm 104:4.

445. On this important point, see *Abbot Columba Marmion*, pp. 232-236.

446. October 8, 1920.

447. Undated.

448. February 13, the year not given. Quoting Hosea 2:20.

449. February 1920.

450. "Hoc est opus Dei ut credatis in eum quem misit Pater." John 6:29.

451. "Hic est Filius meus dilectus, in quo mihi bene complacui: Ipsum audite." Matthew 17:5.

452. Undated.

453. Undated.

454. Thought inspired by Saint Gertrude: "For all Thy gifts to me, my God, and all that memory can recall, in thanks to Thee I give Thee what is Thine own, namely, Thy Divine Heart; to the sweet music of which, resounding through the power of the Holy Spirit, the Paraclete, I sing to Thee, Lord God, adorable Father, praises and thanks on behalf of every creature, of those in heaven, of those on earth and in the depths, and those that are now, or once were, or shall ever be." From *Prayer of Saint Gertrude and Saint Mechtildis*, translated by Rev. John Gray (Sheed and Ward).

455. May 29, 1915.

456. July 1, 1915.

457. Hosea 2:20.

458. October 2, 1919.

459. *Christ, the Life of the Soul*, chap. X, "Prayer."

460. *Christ, the Ideal of the Monk*, chap. XV, § VI.

461. Ibid., p. 360.

462. March 6, 1901.

463. October 5, 1906.

464. April 26, 1909.

465. *Christ, the Life of the Soul,* chap. X, "Prayer," § 4; *Christ, the Ideal of the Monk,* pp. 365 ff.

466. December 5, 1894.

467. May 1, 1915.

468. November 10, 1917.

469. April 19, 1906. Already in 1895 (letter of August), he had recommended the reading of this work which he himself had studied.

470. Letter of May 7, 1917.

471. In *Abbot Columba Marmion,* p. 426.

472. October 5, 1913.

473. May 29, 1915.

474. April 19, 1909.

475. November 15, 1908.

476. Holy Saturday, 1895.

477. January 29, the year not given. [A footnote in the original edition of *Union with God* referred the reader to *Abbot Columba Marmion,* pp. 257-258, for the text of the letter which is reproduced here.]

478. July 23, 1906.

479. This is why we find so little in his letters about ecstatic states and extraordinary mystical prayer.

480. Cf. John 14:21.

481. December 2, 1908.

482. "Universae viae Domini misericordia et veritas." Psalm 24:10.

483. November 1, 1908.

484. "Vivo ego, jam non ego, vivit vero in me Christus." Galatians 2:20.

485. Cf. James 1:17. Letter dated August 31, 1909.

486. December 21, 1908.

487. "OBSECRO vos, filiae Jerusalem, ne suscitetis nec evigilare faciatis dilectam donec ipsa velit." Cf. Canticles 2:7.

488. "Quaerite primum regnum Dei et justitiam ejus et haec omnia adjicientur vobis." Matthew 6:33. Letter dated November 1, 1908.

489. "Haec omnia adjicientur vobis." Matthew 6:33. Letter dated September 6, 1909.

490. November 1, 1908.

491. Allusion to the beginning of the Gospel of Saint John.

492. Cf. 1 Corinthians 1:28-29. Letter dated December 21, 1908.

CHAPTER SIX

493. July 11, 1913.

494. December 17, 1913.

495. Dom Marmion may perhaps seem to exaggerate here the certainty that persons may obtain on the subject of their vocation, but it will be remarked that it is not a question, taken in the concrete, of a theory concerning religious vocation; it is a case rather of keeping a too undecided soul in the path of perfection; any falling off would render her unhappy, fidelity on the contrary, will lead her to the state of life most salutary for her.

496. April 15, the year not given.

497. February 20, 1918.

498. October 14, 1909.

499. January 7, 1910.

500. They figure amongst the earliest we have of Dom Columba.

501. 1 Kings 15 (1 Samuel 15).

502. September 12, 1894.

503. September 16, 1894.

504. October 2, 1894.

505. February 10, 1914.

506. Out of discretion we do not give the date.

507. June 15, 1902.

508. August 19, 1902.

509. "Hic vir perfecit omnia quae dixit illi Deus." Office for Confessors.

510. February 6, 1921.

511. *Rule*, chap. I.

512. February 24, 1913.

513. See the testimony of this religious in *Abbot Columba Marmion*, p. 257.

514. "Imposuisti HOMINES super capita nostra." Psalm 65:12. Saint Benedict utilizes this Scriptural text in his *Rule*, chap. VII.

515. "Ignis consumens." Cf. Hebrews 12:29.

516. "In capite libri scriptum est de me ut faciam Deus voluntatem tuam... Tunc dixi: ECCE VENIO ut faciam voluntatem tuam." Psalm 39: 8-9 and Hebrews 10:5, 7.

517. "Paulus plantat, Apollo rigat, DEUS AUTEM INCREMENTUM DAT." Cf. 1 Corinthians 3:6.

CHAPTER SEVEN

518. The special character of this chapter does not allow of its entering into the order of the plan adopted. These pages are rather in the form of an appendix, but it would certainly have been a regrettable omission not to publish them. It will be seen moreover how Dom Marmion applies to a special category of souls the principles exposed in the course of the preceding chapters.

519. *Rule*, chap. II. See also chap. LXIV.

520. Cf. *Abbot Columba Marmion*, chap. X, "Christ's Representative," and *Christ, the Ideal of the Monk*, p. 47.

521. Cf. *Abbot Columba Marmion*, p. 136.

522. March 7, 1909.

523. March 17, 1918.

524. *Rule*, chap. LXVIII.

525. Undated.

526. Cf. Proverbs 16:25; cf. *Rule*, chap. II.

527. Quoting Saint Francis de Sales, Letter CXLVIII.

528. Cf. Psalm 36:5.

529. Out of discretion we do not give the date.

530. March 17, 1918.

531. March 28, 1904.

532. See chap. II § 1 of this book, "Love, the Principle of Union."

533. "Simon Joannis, diligis me plus hic? Pasce oves meas." John 21:15, 17.

534. "Christus dilexit Ecclesiam et tradidit Seipsum pro ea." Ephesians 5:25.

535. December 16, 1902.

536. February 8, 1901.

537. October 21, 1908.

538. June 5, the year not given.

539. Undated.

540. January 10, 1907.

541. September 7, 1909.

542. January 23, 1909.

543. Undated.

544. November 6, probably 1917.

545. "Scit enim quia his omnibus indigetis." Matthew 6:32.

546. June 1899.

547. November 1, 1908.

548. *Rule*, chaps. II and LXIV.

549. May 17, 1903.

550. March 1, 1918.

551. February 11, 1902.

552. September 1, 1909.

553. Undated, but between 1900 and 1902.

554. "Semper ad Dominum, sicut oculi ancillae in manibus dominae suae." Cf. Psalms 24:15 and 122:2. Letter dated April 11, year not given.

555. *Rule*, chap. II.

556. "In capite libri scriptum est de me ut faciam voluntatem tuam. VOLUI... Ecce venio ut faciam Deus voluntatem tuam. HAC VOLUNTATE SANCTIFICATI SUMUS OMNES." Cf. Hebrews 10:7, 10.

557. "Multorum servire moribus." Cf. *Rule*, chap. II.

558. According to legend, Saint Peter was fleeing Rome to avoid persecution. While on the Appian Way, he met Jesus, and asked Him, *"Domine, quo vadis?"* (Lord, where are You going?) Jesus answered, "I am going to Rome to be crucified again." Shamed, Peter turned around to go back to Rome and martyrdom.

559. March 27, 1920.

560. April 9, 1903.

561. June 1, 1899.

562. March 1907.

563. December 17, 1901.

564. Matthew 12:20 (quoting Isaiah 42:3).

565. "Auferte malum de medio vestri." Cf. 1 Corinthians 5:13.

566. *Rule*, chap. XXVIII. Letter dated December 4, 1917.

567. Undated.

568. *Rule*, chap. LXIV.

569. "Ecce venio ut faciam voluntatem tuam." Cf. Hebrews 10:9.

570. "Iota unum aut unus apex non praeteribit donec OMNIA fiant." Cf. Matthew 5:18.

571. *Ascent of Mount Carmel,* Advice to a religious.

572. September 10, 1913.

573. December 1, 1921.

574. Undated.

575. "Si oculus tuus simplex fuerit, non habens ullam partem tenebrarum, totum corpus tuum lucidum erit et sicut lucerna fulgoris illuminabit te." Luke 11:34, 36.

576. "Ut in omnibus *glorificetur Deus.*" *Rule,* chap. LVII. Letter dated November 23, 1920.

577. 1 Corinthians 1:25.

578. Cf. 1 Corinthians 1:30.

579. Cf. Psalm 36:5. Undated.

580. November 29, 1906.

581. February 20, 1917.

582. "Mea omnia tua sunt." John 17:10.

583. 1906.

584. "Ego sum via, nemo venit ad Patrem, nisi per Me." Cf. John 14:6.

585. November 20, 1916.

586. "Sine me nihil potestis facere." John 15:5.

587. Undated.

588. Allusion to a previous passage in the letter where Dom Marmion mentions the repugnance felt by this Superior to remaining in charge.

589. February 20, 1917.

590. March 17, 1914.

591. "Si diligitis Me, mandata mea servate." John 14:15. Letter dated June 15, 1901.

592. March 15, 1914.

593. At a later period, in a letter of January 1918, he expresses it in this way: "Fidelity in all things is the most delicate flower of love to which nothing is little."

594. "Laus gloriae gratiae suae." Ephesians 1:6. Letter dated December 4, 1906.

INDEX